BLUE JELLY

Love Lost and the Lessons of Canning

DEBBY BULL

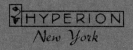

HYPERION
New York

Library of Congress Cataloging-in-Publication Data

Bull, Debby.
   Blue jelly : love lost and the lessons of canning / Debby Bull.
         p.   cm.
   ISBN 0-7868-6255-6
   1. Women—Psychology—Case studies.   2. Separation (Psychology)—Case studies.   3. Man-woman relationships— Case studies.
4. Canning and preserving.   5. Cookery (Jelly)   I. Title.
HQ1206.B83   1997
818'.5409—dc20
[B]   96-30196
                                                               CIP

BOOK DESIGN BY CLAUDYNE BIANCO BEDELL

FIRST EDITION

10 9 8 7 6 5 4 3 2 1

for O.

The author thanks Kyle Ericksen, Jane Swenson, Audrey Hall, Colleen Butler Scissors, Po Bronson, Helene Duban, Ross MacDonald, the extended Bernice and Vernon Jensen family, Bruce Tracy, Terry McDonell, Tom Judson, Andy Weiner, Jann Wenner, Jeremiah Creedon, Roy Bittan, Mike Gregory, the Bohart Ranch, Weller's Books, Margaret Warner, Sean Brooks, Ethel Simonstad, Adam Miller, my editor, Laurie Abkemeier, and especially, Carolyne Fuqua and Regina Torgerson Miller.

CONTENTS

INTRODUCTION *When her boyfriend leaves her, the author discovers the Zen of jelly-making.* 3

1 • CRAB APPLE JELLY *Hiking provides one kind of miracle, crab apples another.* 9

2 • DILL BEANS *The author sits in the desert with a guru and gets more wisdom from a friend.* 21

3 • RASPBERRY JAM *Therapy doesn't work, but the author finds a water slide and the sheer obviousness of jam.* 30

4 • MEXICAN HOT PICKLED VEGETABLES *An attempt at dating again ends in two discoveries: hot pickles, and marriage is not for everyone.* 39

CONTENTS

5 • DANDELION JELLY *A famous New York editor needs a wife. She doesn't get one. Expressing yourself is the point, not getting approval for it, as the blue jelly makes clear.* 49

6 • PLUM JAM *A course in how to have loving relationships requires meeting with some immortalists. Forever. This leaves a lot of time for plums.* 57

7 • RHUBARB JAM *The author goes home to Wisconsin, to the mental hospital.* 66

8 • MOM'S APPLE BUTTER *Everyone draws the line somewhere. Sometimes, luckily, it gets drawn for you.* 74

9 • RED PEPPER JELLY *Collecting lets you leave your own history for a while. Plus, you can make use of all the old jars.* 83

10 • WATERMELON RIND PICKLES *Would a change of scenery help? No, but having people running around in your life does.* 90

CONTENTS

11 • RED CURRANT JELLY *Depression doesn't change the course of history. It just wastes your time.* 98

12 • SPICY MARINATED MUSHROOMS *Despair runs deep. Usually a lot deeper than what just happened. The author discovers that it is harder to get over the Musky Festival than any old boyfriend.* 108

13 • BLUEBERRY BUTTER *An elderly murderess goes to the slammer, and the author breathes a sigh of relief while making a circle tour of Montana.* 118

14 • DILL GREEN TOMATO PICKLES *A trip to India to jump-start a happy new life ends with a big move forward in rubber thongs.* 125

15 • CINNAMON PRUNE MARMALADE *You win some, you lose some, you find the light at the end of the funnel.* 135

CONTENTS

16 • NO ROSEMARY APPLE JELLY
A blue sky of old Ball jars covered one wall, but it was when the author turned her back on them that they did the trick. 141

APPENDIX • BETTER THAN BOTULISM
There are a few things you need to know about canning: questions answered, problems foreseen, shopping lists made. 145

"THERE'S ONLY ONE WAY TO WRITE A SONG,

OR ANYTHING ELSE—

YOU GET ALL WORKED UP

AND THEN YOU TELL THE TRUTH."

—JOE STRUMMER, THE CLASH

I WAS driven to canning by the wreck of my heart. My boyfriend and I were having a dinner party. Our friends had arrived, but he was late. I called him. He said he wasn't coming. Ever. He said he had fallen in love. He said he wanted a divorce, except we weren't even married. I stumbled around and collected his things, even the things that were presents. One Christmas, he'd given me a gold coffee filter. I knew he'd gotten it as a free bonus with his new coffee maker, but I thought it was a tribute to how no-frills I was. I thought of the Valentine's Day when he'd given me a handful of those scent strips you can tear out of magazines.

For weeks, I cried really hard and watched Court TV, thinking about all the lucky people who'd been murdered by the defendants on trial. Then one day I called someone in L.A. and got a wrong number, a man who told me he had just written a country song called, "I'm So Miserable Without You, It's Almost Like I've Got You Back." I was stunned: here was flat-out evidence of a divine presence. "It's a *joke,*" he said, not appreciating the awe. "Not to me," I said.

I became determined to get better. That day, I found a big sack of wild huckleberries that my boyfriend had left in the freezer, and I used them all up making jam. I didn't even know how to make jam. I just didn't want his stuff around. I followed the instructions on the Sure-Jell package, and I couldn't believe it when it worked. Something turned out right, and I took it as a harbinger of my whole future life.

I turned to pickles, stuffing all the string beans from his garden—which, I had to admit, had recently stopped producing anything—into my grandmother's old blue Ball jars. A head of dill, some garlic, a pepper, the brine, and suddenly I had dill beans, which I didn't have to think about again till they were ready at Halloween, one of the few holidays that isn't hard to get through alone. But there was nothing so satisfying as making apple butter. You cook apples into a mush that burbles noisily and hurls wads of itself at the ceiling. You start to wonder why your mom doesn't come in screaming and throw you out of the kitchen.

Canning may sound like a strange path out of the dark woods of despair, but all the other ways, from Prozac to suicide, are really hard on your body. And therapy—breathing new life into the story every week—doesn't always help. When you're really depressed, you have to do something that takes you out of the drama, that makes you detach from the big world and become king of a tiny, controllable world, like one of berries and Ball jars. Just because this last thing didn't work out and your heart is smashed, it doesn't mean that all of your dreams will end in a big mess. Canning demonstrates this principle.

You might argue that you could do other, easier things, like baking. With cookies and cakes, you wind up with something you actually have to eat right now. And there are not enough steps. Canning is a whole world of a thing to do. It requires that you get out of your head. It's a Zen thing. You cannot be wondering about your inadequacies and how they drove Bob off and be making jelly. You'll wind up with big, cylindrical jujubes. You have to be in the moment, paying attention. You boil and sterilize stuff, you time things, you measure and take temperatures: you create an orderly little world. Unlike what has happened to you, these steps take you to what you planned on. You become a person in a world in which things turn out the way you thought they would.

After the huckleberries and the beans and the apple butter, a setback led to things like zucchini bread-and-butter pickles and pickled ginger. When it was over, the jars covered all the counter tops, and I knew I could live through this. I added up all the quarts and pints and half-pints and put the numbers on the refrigerator, like it was the score of a big contest. I had won. And then I gave it away, all the jars sent off to my friends with broken hearts from lost jobs, lost loves, lost chances. It was like a chain letter, sent in Ball jars, and I hoped that if they would keep it going, we wouldn't all be so depressed.

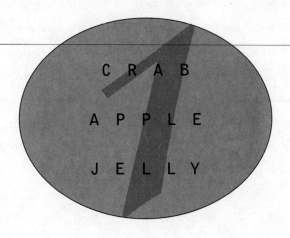

CRAB

APPLE

JELLY

AT CHRISTMAS, I decided it was time to mend fences with my ex-boyfriend. I took a jar of jelly to his house and left it in his mailbox. He pulled into his driveway as I was walking back to my car. He looked at me and he said, "You belong in a mental hospital." He was right: I had to be nuts to want to have anything to do with him.

One of my friends was amazed when I called

her, sobbing all over again: this story defined a theme, she said. When she suspected her live-in boyfriend of more than twelve years of having an affair, she went to the airport to meet his flight. It was his birthday, and she held a little package. He came off the plane holding hands with his girl-friend, and as he walked toward her, he said, "You have finally lost your mind."

Another friend took to the story like Oliver Sacks. "See, it's your depravity that has to be the cause of things," he said, excitedly, "then it's your fall, rather than his fall. Putting the indignity on you is very dishonest." I could tell by the way his voice was cracking that he'd been through this, that it wasn't something just men do after they learn in gym class that the best defense is a good offense. His last girlfriend had tried the same strategy, he said. He could see it all clearly now. He was fine. It had only taken three or four years.

I was so unwound, though, that the suggestion that I go somewhere very quiet made sense. I took to hiking in wilderness areas defined by pleasant green blotches on the map. The fact that the parts you struggled through always ended in some big scenic payoff was an easy analogy to take in. When the snow got too deep, I drove south to a green blotch that still offered hiking, near Cortez, Colorado. I stopped for lunch at a Mexican place that was full of huge plastic gazebos that belonged outside. I was studying a trail map when a man washing dishes in the back came over. He had been disfigured, left with a seriously misshapen jaw, in some sort of an accident. He told me there was a secret spot where he liked to go hiking with his family, and he drew a little map.

It looked to be a very desolate location, but I was curious. Back in the car, I followed his directions to the trail. I walked four or five miles down a red sand path that followed a canyon. It was the desert, and there wasn't much to look at. I was beginning to wonder if I'd taken a wrong turn, and then, suddenly, there were cliff dwellings all around me—a whole city carved in the red rocks. It seemed like a kind of miracle, both the city in the cliffs and the fact that I'd forgotten how kind people can be.

I got a feeling that always made me think of Freddy Fender. I interviewed him when I worked at *Rolling Stone,* and he told me that when he sang, it was to a dream girl in his imagination. His eyes started to fill up with tears, and he said, "Whenever I think of her, I get a frog in my heart."

On my way back to Montana, I pulled off the freeway in Idaho and followed some dirt back roads until I found a turquoise trailer where a woman named Dottie had told me she lived. She was the sister of Charlene Arthur, who was one of the girl Elvises of the fifties. Charlene could've been a bigger star, so I'd been wanting to talk to Dottie about what had happened. I had become transfixed by her, after I'd seen a picture of her leaning against a car, smoking a cigarette, in a fancy Western shirt and pants. That Colonel Tom Parker wanted Charlene to wear a dress was one thing, but Dottie saw a more general pattern of trouble. "You can die trying to get along with a disagreeable man," she said, and I put a star beside it when I wrote it down and then taped it to the rear-view for the rest of the drive. She hadn't said "abusive," I noticed; she had said that just disagreeable could kill you.

When I got home, my neighbor called to ask if I wanted some crab apples, and I carried the canning equipment up from the basement. Crab apples make your hair stand on end if you bite into them raw. They're small and sour and worthless—unless you're making jelly, and then they're tart and full of flavor, easy to jell and cheap to buy. This teaches you that you can be fooled by first impressions. I went to a psychic once and complained about my ex-boyfriend. "You bought a house without checking the foundation," she said. I couldn't believe it. Not only had this guy left, but my house was going to fall apart. "It's a metaphor!" she shouted. "I mean you fell in love before you had his history. Next time, show some restraint."

You get to practice restraint when you make jelly; the juice drips in an agonizingly slow way from the jelly bag, and you just have to wait. Crab-apple juice is a dreamy pink. I've found that when you're really devastated, it's the best color to wear. People don't want to cream you when you're wearing pink. Instead they'll ask you if you need anything, which is probably a far cry from the way Bob was treating you before he left.

HALF-PINT JARS

CRAB APPLES

SUGAR

1. *Wash the crab apples and remove the blossom end. Cut them into quarters. You don't have to peel them or remove the seeds. The aggravating part should never take longer than the pleasurable stuff.*

Barely cover the cut-up apples with water in a wide-bottomed saucepan. An 8- or 10-quart kettle or the bottom of a Dutch oven is good, just so the pan's broad and flat-bottomed for the excess liquid to evaporate quickly. Now boil the fruit until it's truly mushy.

2. *Put this mush in a wet jelly bag and hang it over a bowl. If you don't know what a wet jelly bag is, invent something. It'll make you feel too clever to be in a relationship with a jerk. For example, you can lay three layers of cheesecloth in a bowl, put the crab apples on top and tie the cloth up, like a bag, hanging it up over a bowl to drain off the juice. Let it strain overnight. Sleep. Dream. In the morning, don't squeeze the jelly bag. It probably doesn't sound like something you'd even think of doing, but the bag will be fat and looking like a squeeze*

would make a lot more juice come out. Squeezing, though, makes the jelly cloudy and it's supposed to be clear, and not just for psychological reasons.

3. Wash, then sterilize the jars for 10 minutes in a huge pot of boiling water. Leave them in the hot water till you're ready to use them, or stick them on a tray in the oven to keep them warm. Sylvia Plath, of course, stuck her head in the oven. This is a much healthier use of the gas. Don't throw out the hot water, because you're going to use it later to boil the finished jars of jelly.

Stick all the lids and the rings in a small saucepan with water to cover them all, bring the water just to a boil, then turn off the heat and leave them in the hot water. Very easy: if you're too much of a mess to make the jelly, just stop after everything is sterilized.

4. Measure the juice that dripped from the jelly bag into a saucepan. Then measure out ¾ cup of sugar for each cup of juice, and put all the sugar in a bowl, so that it's ready for you to throw in all at once. Bring the juice to a boil over high heat, and let it go for about 5 minutes.

Add the sugar to the boiling juice, stir to dissolve it, and boil fast to the jelly stage. This is the part where you have to concentrate. You could wreck everything, or you could turn your whole life around. Set a timer, and after about 10 minutes, begin to test for the jelling point.

Dip a big, cold, metal spoon in the pot, raise it a foot out of the steam, let the syrup cool for a couple of seconds, then turn the spoon on its side—the syrup is jelly when, instead of two separate drips at each end of the bowl of the spoon, the liquid runs together in the center of the bowl and makes one big droplet, or glob. This is the "sheeting" test, and it's worth getting the hang of it because it's ridiculous. Here you were cooking something and suddenly you're doing the sort of science experiment Mr. Wizard did with ten-year-olds.

On the other hand, you can use a candy thermometer and cook the jelly to a temperature that's 8 degrees higher than the boiling point of water where you are. At sea level, that's 220 degrees. At 4,000 feet, it's 212 degrees. Please be forewarned: this method sounds easier and it should be the most scientific and reliable, but it always leaves me with hard, overdone jelly wads. One other way—the Refrigerator Test—is to put a spoonful of the syrup on a little plate and stick it quickly into the freezer compartment. Wait a minute, then check it: if it's not liquid when you push it with your finger, but bounces like jelly, it's done.

Please at least try the sheeting test with the big spoon.

5. Remove the boiling syrup from the burner and quickly skim off the foamy scum that forms on the surface. This is extremely sticky, so you want to have a bunch of big clean spoons at hand, because when you try to throw the scum off the spoon, it's usually stuck on to it. You don't have time, at this point, to be too neat, so just hurl the spoon into the sink and use another till you've gotten all the scum out.

Fill the dry, hot jars with the jelly, leaving ¼ inch of headspace, which is the room between the food and the top of the jar rim. Ladle it in through a wide-mouthed funnel, if you have one, which just makes more of the sticky jelly syrup land inside the jar. Wipe the jar rims clean, removing any jelly drips with the tip of a towel dipped in the water that you sterilized the jars in.

6.   Place the hot lids on the jars and screw the rings on firmly. Process in the boiling water canner for 10 minutes. Add one minute for every 1,000 feet that you are above sea level. Friends in Denver boil for 15 minutes, and so on. Count the processing time from the point when the water comes back to a rolling boil after the jars are added.

7.   Pull the jars out of the water with a jar puller. That's really what it's called. Or you can get by with a pair of big tongs. Don't tighten the screw bands afterward or turn the jars upside down. In other words, you have to stop

yourself from thinking that you could have done more.

As the jars start to cool, you will hear what you may think, wishfully, are gunshots in the kitchen. As the lids seal, they pop. After three or four hours, test for a seal on all the jars by poking on the top of the lid; it will be stuck downward if it's sealed. If it wiggles up and down, it didn't seal, and you have to eat it now.

DILL BEANS

2

I WAS told to put my things in the Caravansary of Joy and get right over to the Perceptory of Light. I was checking in at the Institute of Mentalphysics in the California desert. My heart was broken, but it was my mind I was worried about: I couldn't make myself happy anymore. I tried looking for answers everywhere. This time, I joined the audience of a former cable-TV saleswoman who claimed to be possessed by the spirit of a 35,000-year-old man. What the woman was saying when I walked in was, "Is-ness cannot be is not." Hundreds of people sat before her on the floor. She used the sort of language you usually hear only in sci-fi movies where people from other planets speak English, but awkwardly enough to let you know they're not from Earth. She called us *humanoids.* She sat on a throne, looking remarkably like Doris Day. When she finished an idea, she yelled, "So be it!" and everyone yelled, "So be it!" back, like it was a pep rally in the Bible.

I was there for a whole week, and the theme of my week was "To Engage the Knowledge of Individual Destiny," which was exactly what I wanted to know. There was one full-size bed and two sets of bunk beds in my dorm room. One of my roommates was a call girl from Las Vegas. She told me that in a past life she had been choked to death with a dildo. Another roommate wore a blond wig in a Nancy Sinatra style and a muu-muu, and she said she was an incest survivor. I was beginning to think that I wasn't so bad off. Another woman, a real-estate agent from Mississippi, had brought her teen-aged son, and they, too, were assigned to my room. And there was Cara, a strikingly beautiful black woman who said she was a metaphysician. She told me she had written a book called *Don't Let Your Ego Make Promises Your Soul Can't Keep.*

We ate with everybody else in the dining hall, and one morning, at breakfast, I asked a very muscular blond what sort of workout she did. She said, "Every morning, I go for a long swim in my imagination." After that, we tramped through deep sand in a dry river bed to get to a place way out in the desert. "Contemplate your hang-ups and hang-downs," Doris Day said, "then contemplate the sun

23

and the earth. They are forever and grand, and your problems are small."

I winced at Cara. "I came a long way, and this isn't helping," I said. She grabbed my arm, a little too hard, and we walked off together to a hillside.

"You came a long way for the two of us to meet," she said. "Why does your life depend on having that relationship? If one person can disturb you until you want to die, that is just absurd. Having a man is just fun, it's not important. Relationships are here to entertain us, but they're not why we're here—just to bog down in a separate world with one other person. The whole play has to be about something bigger than that."

We sat down on a big rock, watching below as the people who were contemplating their hang-ups walked back to the dorms. "You loved this act so much that you didn't want it to end," she went on, "but it has already stopped. The curtain has closed. It's childish to stomp your feet and cry. Now you have to move into a new act. Maybe there's some piece of the story you have to pick up. And then who's to say he won't be there again in Act Three? There may be something really important for you to learn about the whole thing before he shows up again. You have no idea who's in your life for forever. There is nothing to do except to be excited that the play continues.

"Besides," she added, "how do you even know what you want? You don't even know what's out there."

We were almost back to the Caravansary of Joy. I started singing an old R&B song while we walked up the rest of the path. Cara stopped. She was looking at me in a funny way. "Do you know who wrote that?" she asked. I nodded. He was one of my heroes—one of the great Motown songwriters. "He's my husband," she said, and I remembered how it used to feel when everything seemed to be working out.

On the drive to the airport, I felt high. I saw a sign over a shop that said, "House of Gurus." I understood this new world, felt myself in tune with it. And then as I got closer, I could see that it actually said, "House of Guns."

When I finally got home, string beans were hanging everywhere in the garden. You always wind up with too many beans all at once, like those times when you get a sudden rush of good fortune. You don't question it, but you know it won't last forever. Gardening is always giving up lessons about acceptance of whatever happens. It restores the proper perspective on things. You have your hands in the soil, and as the 35,000-year-old man would say, your problems are small compared to the earth.

QUART JARS

GREEN BEANS, LOTS OF THEM

FOR THE BRINE:

5 CUPS DISTILLED WHITE VINEGAR (5% ACIDITY)

½ CUP PICKLING SALT

5 CUPS WATER

FOR PACKING IN THE JARS:

WHOLE HEADS OF DILL WEED

CHILI PEPPERS

GARLIC CLOVES

1. *Sterilize clean jars for 10 minutes in a pot of boiling water. In a small pan, bring some water just to a boil over the lids and rings, turn off the heat, and leave them in the water until you're ready to use them. Remove the*

jars from the water. Put them upside down to drain for a minute on a pad of clean towels.

2.   *Stick a garlic clove or two, a chili pepper, and a big head of dill on the bottom of each jar. Use half a chili pepper if you don't like things spicy. Pack the beans carefully in the jars, standing them up straight. Take your time. Depending on how long they are, you might have to put a second row on top of the heads of the bottom row. Make sure the beans are really packed in. If they're not tightly packed in, when you're done, the beans float around, adrift, in the finished jars. It's a horrible thing to look at if you think it somehow resembles the way your life is going. If there's room, put another head of dill at the top of the jar.*

3.   *Boil the liquid for the brine in a stainless steel or enamelware saucepan for 3 minutes. There's no mounting pressure here, like with jelly, and if you need more brine for the amount of beans you're pickling, you can*

just stop wherever you are and make more. Pour the brine into each jar, covering the beans with liquid and leaving ½ inch of headspace. If you see air bubbles trapped anywhere in the jar, you can slide a chopstick or a plastic-handled something down the side and release the bubbles. If you've slopped stuff over the side, wipe the rim of the jar clean with the tip of a towel dipped in the hot water that you boiled the jars in.

4. Place the hot lids on the jars and screw the rings on firmly, but not so hard that when you go to open them you cry because there's no man around anymore to open things that are stuck. Process in the boiling water canner for 20 minutes, adding one minute for every 1,000 feet you are above sea level. Count the processing time from the point when the water comes back to a rolling boil after the jars are added.

Wait six weeks or longer for the beans to ripen before you open any of the jars.

RASPBERRY

JAM

3

MY PILLOWCASES were still soggy from tears
and covered in smudged mascara. A friend recom-
mended her therapist, so I got an appointment and
went to see Donna. I told her the scenario: while
he'd written a novel, I'd taken care of everything
else. I bought the food, mowed the lawn, cleaned
the house, edited his book, and finally, all my sav-

ings were gone. I could hardly stand the story: I was so stupid.

I sobbed as I related the whole thing, especially the part about how he'd phoned in the news of our break-up during a party to celebrate the publication of his novel, which was dedicated to me in a careful wording, like a clause in a contract you know you want to back out of.

Donna quietly took it all in. At the end, she leaned forward in her seat and stared at me thoughtfully. "Have you seen *The Little Mermaid?*" she asked. I cocked my head, hoping I hadn't heard right. "It's the story of a girl who loses her voice," she said, "and I think that's what happened to you."

I marveled that there was a whole new branch of psychotherapy that matched your case up with the right Disney cartoon, but I felt I was more of a Dumbo and I never went back.

A friend called from L.A. and listened intently to my story. "I can't see my shrink anymore either," she said. I thought she meant that she also had gotten nowhere. She said that she thought she was making progress, until she started dating a soap-opera actor. She was crazy about him, and he seemed sort of serious about her, too. Then he suddenly stopped calling. She related this all to her therapist, a woman who looked ashen as she wrapped it up. Her shrink knew what was wrong. She said, "I'm going out with him."

I didn't need a therapist to tell me that part of the problem was that I got all my ideas about love from rock & roll records. My all-time favorite was the Jackson 5's "I Want You Back," and it might as well have played behind every love scene of my life. When I was a teenager in northern Wisconsin, if it was nighttime and there weren't a lot of clouds and you were in a car with a long antenna on top of a hill, you could pull in WLS out of Chicago. They had an hour when they played early rhythm & blues records, and the best one was Claudine Clark's "Party Lights." Real happiness is out of reach in that song, something you can hear but you can't quite get near; love is a party that you're not invited to. Misery and longing were stuck in my ideas about romance. I would become "A Fool in Love" and be like Tina Turner.

Just to listen to the radio, especially to the country songs that now seemed profound, I decided to go for a long drive through Wyoming. I pulled off the road when I came to a town called Thermopolis. It sounded warm. At the end of the street, there was a place to soak in hot springs, with a big sign that twinkled in the sun and said THE STAR PLUNGE. There were lots of different pools inside, and at the top of a stairwell, there was a small hole to climb through into a long blue tube that wasn't much bigger around than your body laid out flat. I'd never been on a water slide.

A teen-aged boy stopped me from going back

down the stairs. "You just have to relax and take the twists and turns as they come," he said. I'd gotten so used to looking for psychological advice that it took me a minute to see he was talking about the slide. He was right: if you stiffened up and tried to avoid the big dips, you got hammered into the sides; if you weren't trying to hang on, even the sudden falls were fun. I knew the trick was keeping it up when you weren't wearing a bathing suit.

I made a big loop into Utah, where the world just feels a little more orderly, and headed home through Idaho. I pulled off the highway when I saw a sign that said "World Museum of the Potato." First I was directed to go to a service station, where the man at the cash register handed me a coupon for one free russet potato. Then, sadly, out of nowhere, he said, "It's a month to the day that my girlfriend left me." He told me the whole story while we ate some jo-jo's, which were probably covered near the end of the potato history, and from what he said, she sounded awful. "Why would you stay with somebody who treated you like that?" I said, sheepish about asking a question I couldn't answer myself. Then I went to the potato museum, tried the hand lotion made of potatoes, and saw that it was the ending and not the beginning of some relationships that ought to restore your sense of hope.

When I got home, the raspberry bushes had practically shriveled up. Gardening was beginning to teach me to accept sudden changes, the way things come and go. In my garden especially, nothing lasts forever. Some things bear fruit, though, and you can preserve it. You can actually make something last. Raspberry jam is really easy.

Jam is done when it's thick. It doesn't have to cook forever. You don't have to test it; you just look at it and know. Once, I followed a turn-of-thecentury recipe with instructions that said nothing but "Boil raspberries and sugar and put it in jars." Everything is really pretty obvious. I mean, I knew it was over way before that dinner party.

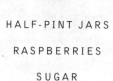

HALF-PINT JARS

RASPBERRIES

SUGAR

1. Put the raspberries in a wide saucepan. If you grew the raspberries yourself, add 10 points. Work with a small amount at a time—like maybe 4 or 5 cups, and no more. Don't get in over your head. Mash the berries to get some juice out. Simmer for half an hour or so or until the berries are really soft, stirring to keep it all from frying on the bottom.

I filled up lots of free time, like when there's nothing to do but stir, thinking about how everything would've turned out perfectly and nobody would've left me if I were prettier. I tried to force myself to think about something Tina Turner had told me. "You cannot put me in the pile with the pretty ones, but I do not go in the pile with the ugly ones, either," she'd said. "And I like it here in the middle. There's a lot more freedom."

Meanwhile, sterilize the jars for 10 minutes in boiling water. Leave them in the hot water till you're ready to use them. In a little saucepan, bring water to a boil over the lids and rings, and turn off the heat.

2. Measure the berry mush. This makes a mess, but you have to do it, even if it means measuring it out into a bowl and then dumping it back into the saucepan. I mean, that you now have an extra bowl to wash is probably the least of your problems. Add an equal amount of sugar to the berries back in the pan.

3. Boil the sugar and raspberries together, stirring well, until the syrup is really sticky and thick, which will prob-

ably be about 20 minutes. Skim off any foamy scum on the top. Throw out the scum. If you follow no other instruction, do this one. Fill the dry, hot jars with the jam, leaving ¼ inch of headspace, and you can be neatest about this if you use a wide-mouthed funnel.

4. Wipe the jar rims clean with the tip of a towel dipped in the boiling water. Place the hot lids on the jars and screw the rings on firmly. Process in the boiling water canner for 10 minutes.

MEXICAN HOT PICKLED VEGETABLES

4

I THOUGHT it might help to start seeing somebody new, to date again. I met the country singer
in the airport in Denver, and he left me months
later in the airport in Austin, Texas. One night in
between, he phoned to sing me a song he'd just
written. It was called, "This One's Gonna Hurt
You for a Long, Long Time." You could say I was

warned. By the time it was a hit on the radio, I got the cosmic joke.

Not long after we'd met, he suggested a road trip across the hill country of south Texas. We stayed in motels that had been decorated by taxidermists and ate in Denny's, where waitresses would ask for his autograph. He wasn't that famous yet, but he dressed the part anyway, making me think all the time of all those birds that have a drab female and a brightly plumed male. He was from the South, and he said things like, "What's time to a hog?" which, it turned out, had nothing to do with the town we stopped in that was the Home of the Swimming Pig. It was hot outside, and he would say, "I just saw a dog chasin' a rabbit and both of 'em were walkin'."

We stopped at both the Alamo and a replica of it called the Alamo Village, where John Wayne had made movies, and he'd suddenly whip out a notebook and write down lines he'd thought of for new songs, asking me what I thought of them. We traveled together for a week, and though it was very clear that what he wanted was not a relationship but some new material, I cried my heart out when he didn't call after I got home.

Not long after that, his record came out. There was a song called "Easy to Love (Hard to Hold)," which explained everything. But there was another called "Don't Leave Her Lonely Too Long," and one day he called again, like he'd never been gone. This sort of thing went on for a while, and it never occurred to me to ask what was going on. I guess I was waiting for more concrete evidence that this was not a perfect relationship, like when the girlfriend of one of my friends made an appearance on *The Tonight Show,* and she said she wished she could meet someone she could really care about.

I had a hard time letting relationships go, even the ones I didn't like. When it was finally over with

41

the country singer, my friends tried to console me by pointing out how weird the country singer dressed, like he was Roy Rogers, but that had been one of his best qualities.

I decided to drive all the way from Montana to see the real Roy Rogers, who was in his eighties, at his museum in Victorville, California. Roy was never as rich as Gene Autry, the other big singing cowboy, and I knew there'd been tragedies in his life, like when one of his daughters had been killed in a church bus accident. His life had gone way up and back down, and still, he felt like putting on those fancy cowboy shirts. His story was inspiring: a good life doesn't necessarily go blithely along.

The museum was full of all of Roy and Dale Evans's stuff, like a big attic. Bullet the dog was barking at a critter in a diorama, and even Trigger was stuffed and doing a trick up on his back legs. Roy was waiting in his office when I got there.

Before we began to talk, he said he needed to call Dale. The line was busy, and Roy looked worried. "Who could she be talking to?" he asked. They have about a hundred grandchildren, and I suggested that maybe it was one of them. Roy started to tell me about his hunting trips years ago with Alfalfa from *Our Gang,* but he was staring at the telephone. "I better go home and see if she's okay," he said at last, and he left. I sat there awhile, realizing that though I sometimes thought a marriage like Roy and Dale's was the end-all, I could no more picture myself in one like that than I could see Alfalfa with a gun.

When the country singer and I were in south Texas, we crossed the border into Mexico. On the table in the café where we had dinner was a gallon jar of hot pickled vegetables. On the wall, there was a picture of Annie Oakley. She'd gotten famous when she won a big sharp-shooting contest when she was a teenager, and afterward, she'd married the man who lost. She looked really miserable. Lots of married people do. It's a fact you can sometimes console yourself with, when you're alone. Once I went to a massage therapist, who told me she'd felt devastated on her wedding day. "I looked at myself in the mirror," she said, "and I thought, 'Now I'll never get to join the army.'"

When I got back to my house, I figured out how to make Mexican relish. You can make it so hot it makes your eyes water, though I was beginning to feel like I'd cried enough.

PINT JARS

1 CAULIFLOWER, BROKEN INTO FLORETS

1 RED SWEET PEPPER, CUT IN STRIPS

2 OR 3 CUPS BABY CARROTS OR THINLY
SLICED ADULT CARROTS

BLUE JELLY

2 CUPS CELERY, CUT IN INCH-LONG SLICES

2 CUPS SMALL WHOLE ONIONS OR 2 MEDIUM
ONIONS, QUARTERED

PICKLING SALT

PICKLING SOLUTION:

5 CUPS DISTILLED WHITE VINEGAR (5% ACIDITY)

1 CUP WATER

$\frac{1}{2}$ CUP SUGAR

FOR PACKING IN JARS:

CHILI PEPPERS, DRIED OR FRESH

GARLIC CLOVES

1. *After you've cut them up, put all the vegetables into a stoneware, pottery, or glass bowl (not a metal one). Cover with water and sprinkle with ¼ cup pickling salt.*

Don't use table salt. Stir the salt into the water and mix it up well with the vegetables.

Make sure all the vegetables are covered in the liquid. You can put a plate on top to sink the vegetables under the water. Leave it alone for an hour or more.

The country singer was not the first about-to-be-famous guy I'd gone out with: once, in the middle of an interview for Rolling Stone, a comedian leaned over and kissed me. It was unprofessional to kiss him back, but it felt exactly like I'd fallen headfirst onto a pillow. He had the softest lips. We went out a few times, and then one night, right across from me, a beautiful waitress sat down in his lap and passed a piece of paper with her phone number on it into his mouth with her tongue. I didn't see him anymore. In a notebook in my apartment, he'd written down the line "a dog named Stay," and by the time it was a joke on TV, it made people go crazy.

Drain the vegetables.

2. Wash, then sterilize the jars for 10 minutes in boiling water. Leave them in the hot water till you're ready to use them. Bring some water to a boil over the lids and rings in a small pan, then turn off the heat, and leave them in the water.

3. For the pickling solution, combine the vinegar, the water, and the sugar in a saucepan that's stainless steel or enamel. Slowly bring to a boil over medium heat, then let it simmer for 15 minutes.

4. Place one chili pepper and a garlic clove in each jar. Pack the vegetables into the hot jars, getting an assortment of all the kinds of vegetables in each jar. You need a little of everything. Pour the hot pickling solution over the vegetables, leaving ½ inch of headspace. If you fill the jar all the way to the top, goo bubbles out when you boil it. Wipe the rim of the jar with a clean towel.

5. *Place the hot lids on the jars and screw the rings on. Process in the boiling water canner for 15 minutes. Count processing time from the point when the water comes back to a rolling boil after the jars are added. You really have to do this for the whole time, or you could kill all your dinner guests with botulism poisoning, go to jail, and your ex-husband's friends will think he was a genius to leave you.*

6. *Make sure the jars are sealed and put them in a cool, dark place. Allow 6 weeks for the pickles to ripen, then give them away.*

DANDELION

JELLY

5

WHEN I still hadn't wholly recovered, I imagined that I would feel better if I really plunged into a job, the kind where you go to an office every day and don't have time to think about other things. I took one with a notorious woman editor in New York. My job was to read the manuscripts that arrived by the pile every day at her office. Most of them promised to be exactly like a John Grisham novel, only the black-female one or the funny-medical one. A twenty-year-old man sent the thirteen crime novels he'd written. In a cover letter, he explained that his mother had been nuts and that after a long separation, she'd turned up again, working at a cuckoo-clock company. It was the only interesting thing I read. Someone else sent a book called *Hung Jury*. It was about penis size.

I was working on my own book, a true crime story, and the editor kept promising to talk to me about it. Finally, she said we could talk about it over dinner at her apartment one evening. I showed up at seven and was surprised that another woman was also there for dinner. The editor was on the phone in her bedroom. Things were a mess, so the other woman, a TV producer, and I began to straighten up a little. At ten-thirty, the editor was still on the phone. We had moved all the paintings and the furniture in the apartment. The producer went home to eat. I was getting my coat when the editor finally came out of her room.

"Don't leave!" she cried. We sat down on the sofa. I told her I was not only going home, I was going back to Montana. "But you have to stay," she pouted. "The apartment looks wonderful! I need you to be my wife."

I was annoyed. "Be your own wife," I said crossly.

I decided to take the opportunity to tell her about my book—about a kid from my hometown in the Midwest who killed his whole family. She was transfixed. It looked like she was reading something over my shoulder. "It's a million seller," she said at last.

I was ecstatic.

"Be Your Own Wife," she said slowly, trying out the title. "You could have a whole line of cleaning products to sell on QVC," she added. Then the phone rang. "This will be so helpful for women

like me," she said, going back into the bedroom.

I went back to Montana, where it was spring, and there were dandelions in the yard. They looked like marigolds. Instead of using weed killer, I picked them to make jelly. There were always a couple ways of seeing things, I was learning.

Still, I wondered why the book thing hadn't panned out. Work sometimes seemed to bring the same rejection as my relationships. I dug around in my bag and found Cara's phone number. "You have to not care whether they approve of you or not," she said when I called. "We do what we do to express ourselves, not to coincide with what others like. You're lucky if they like anything you do."

I was picking the green bottoms off the dandelion tops while we talked and thinking it was like I had my own private Oprah. "Write the story whether anyone wants it or not," she said. "Stop worrying if somebody wants you, and *you* just want you." Then she hung up.

When it came to the part in the jelly recipe where you put in the food coloring, I was out of yellow, so I put in the blue instead. There was something about the blue jelly that seemed perfect, and maybe it was just that nobody else would've liked it.

HALF-PINT JARS

1 QUART DANDELION BLOSSOMS

1 QUART WATER

1 PACKAGE (1¼ OUNCES) POWDERED PECTIN

2 TABLESPOONS LEMON JUICE

4½ CUPS SUGAR

YELLOW FOOD COLORING

1. Pick the dandelion blossoms. Obviously, you don't want to do this after a fresh application of weed killer.

You can't rinse off fertilizer or weed killer, so you may want to gather the dandelions from the yard of your neighbors with the tie-dyed clothes. Hold each flower by its calyx, the green base, and snip off the yellow blossom. Throw away the green part. Boil the blossoms and water in a large saucepan for about 3 minutes.

Wash, then sterilize the jars for 10 minutes in boiling water. Leave them in the hot water till you're ready to use them. In a small pan, bring water to a boil over the lids and rings, turn off the heat, and leave them in the water until you're ready to use them. I always used to quit here, after I got all the stuff sterilized, and lie on the floor and cry. The editor I had worked for was going through a lot, but she never cried. This seemed to scare people—a woman who didn't break down—and no one ever wanted to argue with her.

It wasn't that she wasn't feminine, either. She was really beautiful, and she had a whole closet full of gowns. I'd never had a single dress that was that fancy. She was the editor of a famous radio personality, and to humor him, she often went with him to big events. She told me that it was just work, but that she let him kiss her anyway, passionately and on the lips, when he brought her home. I asked her why she kissed him, and she said, "Because he is a really, really good kisser." She came out ahead in every deal she made.

2. Drain off 3 cups of the dandelion liquid and put it in a wide-bottomed saucepan. Measure out the sugar into a bowl, so you can heave it in all at once. Add the pectin and the lemon juice to the liquid in the pan and bring it to a rolling boil. Throw in all the sugar and the food coloring. You can add any color, really. Yellow just makes the jelly look like dandelions. Boil about 3 minutes to the jelly stage. Use the spoon test to make sure it's done. Remove the boiling syrup from the heat and skim off any foam. Fill the dry, hot jars with the jelly, leaving ¼ inch of headspace.

Another thing you can do is put flowers in, like a petunia or a pansy. This can be annoying, though, because they usually float back up to the top. You may not want to get involved in this, but you can hold the flower down until the jelly starts to thicken. I find it soothingly mind-numbing to attempt to weight a pansy down on the bottom of each jar with a chopstick, then balance the chopstick so it doesn't float out or move, and then pull it out at just the right time. You can lose a whole Saturday night this way.

3. Wipe the jar rims clean with the tip of a towel dipped in the boiling water bath. Place the hot lids on the jars and screw the rings on firmly. Process in the boiling water canner for 10 minutes. Don't tighten the screw band afterward or turn the jars upside down. Give the jelly away when you're done.

P L U M

J A M

"I'M REALLY despondent, but I'm feeling optimistic about it," said a woman in a sunny yellow
dress, up at the microphone during the first night
of the Loving Relationships workshop. I had signed
up for a weekend that promised to improve my relationships.

The people around me were chatting about
the other seminars they'd taken, saying one was

more self-actualizing than another. A man and a woman were on stools in the front of the room. They asked us to identify the first person in the room that we'd looked at. This was to be our buddy for the whole weekend, and they said this would turn out to be the person we had the most in common with. I watched dark-haired women in their thirties introduce themselves to other dark-haired women in their thirties, while I met my own buddy, a seventeen-year-old male ballet dancer named Jeb, whose mother had made him come.

The people on the stools told us that you keep repeating the circumstances of your birth for your whole life. I was born with the cord wrapped around my neck, and one of the stool people said, "I bet you always struggle to get started." He told me that writing the sentence over and over, "I no longer need entanglements in order to feel alive," would help me.

Jeb had been premature, and he was told to

write the sentence, "I no longer have to rush to make it." He said his father was like Archie Bunker, but without the polish. The woman on the stool said, "You do not have to pick through the garbage while it's on the way to the dump." The audience applauded. "Anything unresolved with your parents will come up in your own relationships for the purpose of healing and release," she said, and it didn't look like good news to anybody.

We were told that you have to announce to the universe that you want something, even a new boyfriend. They asked us to write down what we were looking for in a relationship and to put at the bottom of the page, "This or something better now comes to me, in easy and pleasurable ways, with good to all concerned. Thank you, God!"

The Loving Relationships workshop ended with everyone spread out on the floor, panting together for fifteen minutes. This was called "rebirthing." After our rebirth, the people on the stools gave us a list of things we should do, and one was "Join a group of immortalists."

I didn't know a single immortalist, let alone a group of them, and I didn't feel like going to their meetings forever. Still, I made an appointment to meet the woman who'd invented the workshop.

There was Louis Vuitton luggage all over her hotel room. It clued the universe, the woman explained to me, that she deserved an abundance of everything. "Besides, I need to change my clothes," she said, "because a lot of negativity collects on me." She said that she had spent two years in a hot tub perfecting the technique of rebirthing. "It was then that I had a major a-ha," she said to me. "It was that there's a direct correlation between people's births and their relationships." She had written a bunch of popular books, and she said, "The year I came out as a public figure, I would actually walk around feeling my head being pushed out of the birth canal."

I told her I was trying to get over a broken heart. "I can tell that the script at your conception was 'I'm not wanted,' " she said. "So now you have to let a lot of God in, to support the thought that you really are wanted," she added. "And you really should do something about that suicidal impulse." Then she handed me a big color picture of herself, autographed like she was a movie star.

I grabbed a cab, and on the way out of the city, we got stuck in traffic. The driver was eyeing a blond woman in the car beside us. I could see that he was from the Middle East, and I asked him if he liked American women. "Not anymore," he said, looking at me in the rear-view. "Now, I only go out with Egyptians, like myself." He said he had a theory that if there is a great difference between the two people in a relationship, there is a potential for abuse. My ex-boyfriend was younger, and when he got angry, he called me an old hag. We came up with a hundred examples, like a really rich woman I knew who treated her husband like he was the handyman, and when we got to the airport, we hugged each other hard. I imagined it was exactly how the Loving Relationships weekend was supposed to end.

When I got back to Montana, a man in a pickup was selling boxes of fresh Washington fruit, and I bought some plums. When I was a child, my mother had awakened me in the middle of the night for an eclipse, and she'd handed me a photo negative to look through and a sack of plums. The disappearance of the moon and plums were linked to me after that, together with my father in the negative, black now, holding up a dead duck.

Different kinds of plums make different-colored jams, but they are all great colors—deep purple, hot pink, or burgundy. The plum, plain, is not such a great eating fruit, but it makes a tart, smooth jam. In canning, the best stuff comes out of things that aren't so sweet, and you have to hope the analogy covers everything.

PINT OR HALF-PINT JARS

4 CUPS CHOPPED, PITTED PLUMS

3 ½ CUPS SUGAR

1. *Put the cut-up plums in a big saucepan. If you have a lot more plums than what turns into 4 cups, you have to make the jam in batches, so you can work with small amounts at a time. This seems to go against the best advice I ever heard. One night, driving across the country, I got the Reverend Ike from Harlem on the radio. He said,*

"You can go to the ocean with a spoon, or you can go to the ocean with a pail—the ocean don't mind."

Add ½ cup water, cover, and simmer for 5 minutes, to begin breaking down the fruit. Stir in the sugar and let this stand for an hour or two, or even overnight, if you need to rest.

2. Wash, then sterilize the jars for 10 minutes in boiling water. Leave them in the hot water till you're ready to use them. Bring water to a boil over the lids and rings and leave them in the water, too. You always do this step when you're canning, and it's good to think of it, like other small rituals, as calming, rather than so boring you almost want to forget about canning.

3. Over medium or medium-low heat, let the plum and sugar mixture slowly come to a boil, stirring a lot. Keep stirring and cooking for about 20 minutes. I never could get into writing the sentence about entanglements over and over, though you'd have time right here for it.

Before I knew about affirmations, I went into the bathroom at a dentist's apartment in New York, and the walls were carpeted in a fuzzy shag. When you turned on the light, the radio came on, and there was a Post-it note on the mirror that said, "You're beautiful!" I was flattered, but now I think maybe he was talking to himself.

The plum mixture should be pretty thick now. Put a little on a plate in the freezer for a minute. If it's pretty firm, like jelly, it's done.

4. *Skim off any foam from the top. Ladle the jam into the hot, sterilized jars, filling to ¼ inch below the rim. Wipe the jar rims clean with the tip of a towel dipped in the boiling water bath. If you don't clean the rims this way, you might not get a seal.*

5. *Place the hot lids on the jars and screw the rings on firmly. Process in the boiling water canner for 5 minutes, adding one minute for every 1,000 feet above sea level.*

RHUBARB
JAM

I DECIDED that I needed to go back to where I was from for a while: see Wisconsin and my past in a more optimistic light, even though *USA Today* had just announced in a colorful pie chart that people from Wisconsin were the only ones in the country who were fatter and drinking more beer than they were ten years ago.

I planned to stop off for a face-to-face meeting with the kid from my town who had shot and killed his whole family after a childhood of emotional abuse. The teen-aged boy is in the state mental hospital. We'd been writing to each other, and I thought it might make me feel better if I saw what it was like to be in an institution. If it didn't shock me into feeling better, I could just completely fall apart and they could keep me.

The boy told me to bring take-out food, that we could eat together, and I carried it in little Chinese-food containers, which they went over with one of those wands before letting me in. The hallways were painted bright yellow and the floors were grass green, and it seemed a little giddy for a prison. "You're going to kill me," I said when I realized I'd forgotten the soy sauce, and I wished I could take it back.

After we got locked together in a little room,

we started to talk about the landmarks in our hometown, like the high school, which has a fat angel for the team mascot, and the Dairy Queen. Every spring, they have a sign when you enter the town that says something like, "The dilly and his friends are back!" and you go there even though it's always too cold for ice cream. We talked about these places fondly, though I could tell that for both of us, the thought of them floated over a pool of bad memories from when we actually lived there.

The boy told me about his uncle, "an older guy," and I realized he had been in my class. He wore a Future Farmers of America jacket to school every day. The boy said his uncle had been married twice. I started to cry. He was locked up for the rest of his life, but I could only think about the fact that I didn't have even one husband. "Not one of my relationships ever works out," I said, sobbing.

He looked stunned. "At least you get to try," he said, and I had to admit it was a good argument. As we walked to the door, a nice man said hello. I was starting to think that maybe I shouldn't have blown off the whole mental-hospital idea. "He's a serial killer," the boy whispered. "He's helping me do some inner-child work." My ex-boyfriend had tried inner-child work but said he found out he had a whole inner kindergarten.

When I left, I drove with my head out the window, like a dog. Driving north through Wisconsin, I listened to *The Dan Mack Show,* a call-in program for troubled teenagers. Kids describe things like how their mothers make them live in closets and eat cat food, and Dan calls them "buddy" and tells them they'll be okay. Then elderly people call in and offer to pray for the kids. Somehow it actually seemed to help, and I felt a wave of guilt. I had left my answering machine on for months. Even when I was there, I pretended I was gone. It was small, but I promised myself I'd start answering my phone and telling people that they would be okay.

Just before I got to my hometown, I passed a farm I used to go to with my father. He drove a Cadillac convertible—he loaned it out all the time so that queens could ride in it in parades—and in the early summer, we'd wheel into this farm and pick sacks full of rhubarb. One time they told him no, and the next time we went, he told me that he had just bought the whole farm. Rhubarb has leaves like an elephant's ears, but it's the pink stalks that you use in canning. As rhubarb matures, these stalks get stringy and bitter, which ought to have taught me long ago that some things just go sour in time and you can't keep it from happening.

HALF-PINT JARS

5 CUPS RHUBARB

2 ORANGES

5 CUPS SUGAR

1 TEASPOON GROUND CINNAMON

½ TEASPOON GROUND CLOVES

1. Cut a bunch of rhubarb stalks into pieces. Make sure the rhubarb is young. In other words, pull out stalks with smaller, newer leaves instead of the huge-leafed big stalks. Rhubarb is maybe the most humble thing you can grow, but you can make a million things out of it.

2. Peel the oranges and run them through a blender or food processor to grind them up—not the peels, the oranges. Wash, then sterilize the jars for 10 minutes in boil-

ing water. Leave them in the hot water till you're ready to use them. Bring water to a boil over the lids and rings and leave them there.

3. Cook the rhubarb and oranges with the sugar over a low heat, slowly bringing the mixture to a boil. Add the cinnamon and the cloves, if you want a spicier jam; if not, relax. Cook for about 35 minutes, until it's thick but not cement. Stir it up, to quote the late Bob Marley.

I interviewed Marley a long time ago, and between the heavy accent and the fact that he started every sentence, "I and I," I couldn't understand a word he said, so we sat in a room, the tape recorder going, and ate a big bowl full of oranges. Even though I stopped asking him anything, he didn't seem to want to go anywhere, and I certainly didn't. His wife, Rita, came in for a minute and when she left, I said, "Was that your wife?" He smiled and said, "All my wife." Or something. I knew he meant he loved us all and that things probably weren't so easy for Rita. Remove the boiling syrup from the heat *and skim off the foam. If you happen to get some scum in a jar, gently skim it off with a teaspoon.*

4. Fill the dry, hot jars with the jam, leaving ¼ inch of headspace. Wipe the jar rims clean with the tip of a towel dipped in the boiling water bath. Place the hot lids on the jars and screw the rings on firmly. Process in the boiling water canner for 10 minutes.

MOM'S APPLE BUTTER

WHEN I reached my mother's house, there were apples all over the ground in the orchard. Though we never talked that much, we made apple butter, and I marveled at how carefully and patiently she did everything, like we were doing lab work. For the first time ever, she told me that the happiest years of her life were after she got divorced. My father was handsome, but he had an explosive temper. I told her that once I'd overheard a woman talking about finally drawing the line, saying, "I told him that if he ever hits me again, in my face, with his fist, I will leave."

Still, my father was dynamic, and he had dreamed up a hugely successful restaurant made out of an actual steamboat. The billboards along the highway said, "Take a Pleasure Cruise and Relax in the Famous Marine Bar at the Steamboat 'Round the Bend." I had always worked as a waitress for my father, and my attitude about relationships had a lot to do with providing good service. Later, when he remodeled, the old restaurant doors came home, and you could look into other rooms through portholes. It was just like we were on the *Titanic*.

My mother was Scandinavian, and our house had all the fun of a Bergman movie. She had studied chemistry in college, and in the old canning booklet that she'd given me, she'd written down the calculations, year by year, since the fifties, of how many pounds of apples and sugar she'd used and what the exact yield had been. It looked like a lot of pointless figuring, but I knew from my experience that all the pages of numbers probably represented some rare times of calm.

One of my old neighbors had become an Amway salesman, and he gave me a tape to listen to while I drove west. It was a speech somebody had delivered at one of their rallies. The Amway leader said that to get anyone to believe in you, you have to remember three things: feel, felt, and found. "I know how you feel," he said, explaining how you have to say it. "I've felt that way myself. And this is what I've found." "Canning," I said in my head, trying to sound as excited as the guy on the tape.

Back in Montana, I was thinking about the fact that my apple butter would never be as good as my mother's, wondering if a flair for cooking was always in direct proportion to the time spent in a bad relationship, when the doorbell rang. I peeked out the window. A man who was at least eighty was standing there, and I noticed that he had ironed his checked shirt and blue jeans and put a bandana around his neck. I was touched that anybody would bother that much with his appearance. I'd been wearing the same sweatshirt for, like, three months, and grief was only part of it.

I got this from my father. He only wore one outfit: tan khakis and a white cotton T-shirt. It sounds sort of James Dean now, but even the salesmen, who stood around drinking martinis in our bar, wore suits. The worst of it was that my father was always fresh from, say, fixing the dishwasher, and more than once, some salesman would suggest to the bartender that the cleaning man had just stolen a rum and soda. My father couldn't have cared less, and only men of this devout insouciance appealed to me.

While I worked at the magazine, I'd gone out with a suitably sloppy guy, another editor, for about a year, though we kept it to ourselves. One day, the head of my department called me into her office. She was crying, and she said she had to tell me a secret. She said that for a year she had been seeing someone who worked with us. She told me who it was. I had the same secret. I never really liked going to work after that, and though his career took off and he got a job on TV, I saw that he had developed a nervous tic that made him wiggle his head when he talked.

And I wound up in Montana. I'd bought a house there before I knew anyone. I had been desperate to leave New York, the noise and the dirt and the loneliness. As I drove the U-Haul west, I remember passing all the little towns with names like Moccasin and Pony and the big empty spaces in between and knowing that this was going to be equally tough, but in all new ways. I was right. Though just doing normal things like driving to the store had made me feel less daily anxiety, I'd found even more loneliness and people dressed like Howdy Doody.

"I live over there," the man at the door said, pointing down the street. "I brought you something." Then he handed me a bag of lettuce and a government pamphlet on the importance of leafy green vegetables, and out of the blue, he told me he'd pray for me, like we were on *The Dan Mack Show*.

I closed the door. Other people got husbands and children; I got a bag of lettuce. I hurled myself on the floor and sobbed. The worst thing about trying to get myself undepressed were the days when it seemed like I hadn't made any progress at all.

PINT JARS

APPLES, ABOUT 2 DOZEN OF ANY COOKING
VARIETY, LIKE JONATHAN OR WINESAP

SUGAR, WHITE OR BROWN

CINNAMON

CLOVES

ALLSPICE

1. *Wash the apples, core them, and remove the stems. Cut into quarters or eighths. Don't peel them. The pectin, the thing that makes the jelly jell, is concentrated in the skin of the fruit. Add as little water as you can to get the apples started cooking without burning them on the bottom of the pan: try just a half-cup. Putting in as little as you can may be a switch. Let the water simmer and begin to cook the apples, then kind of mash them down when they start to soften.*

2. Wash, then sterilize the jars for 10 minutes in boiling water. Leave them in the hot water till you're ready to use them, or put them on a metal tray in a hot oven. Pour boiling water over the lids and rings and leave them in the water.

3. When the apples are cooked to the point where they are really mushy, like after an hour, put them through a Foley food mill. You can also use a fine sieve. Cranking stuff through the food mill is fun, though, and I can't imagine that pressing the apples through a sieve would be.

4. Measure the strained fruit, and for every cup of pulp, add ½ cup of sugar. Mix that together in a big saucepan or kettle, and add 2 teaspoons of cinnamon, 1 teaspoon cloves, ½ teaspoon allspice, or half that amount if you don't like such strong spices. Eat some to see if you've got it right. Trust your judgment.

5. Cook this mixture over low heat, stirring until the sugar is dissolved. Continue cooking over low heat for

about an hour. You can talk on the phone while you stir. If you don't have any friends anymore because they couldn't stand to see the way that guy treated you, just stir and think about that. Near the end, you have to stir frequently to be sure the apple butter doesn't burn on the bottom of the pan. At this point, it starts hitting the ceiling. At least this is a mess you can clean up without therapy. It's ready when it's really thick and when you put a blob of it on a plate, no ring of water seeps out around the edge.

6.   Fill the dry, hot jars with the apple butter, leaving ¼ inch of headspace. Wipe the jar rims clean with the tip of a towel dipped in the boiling water bath. Place the hot lids on the jars and screw the rings on firmly. Process in the boiling water canner for 5 minutes (add a minute for every 1,000 feet above sea level). Don't tighten the screw band afterward or turn the jars upside down or anything else. It's over.

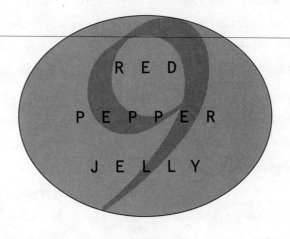

RED
PEPPER
JELLY

ONE DAY I was visiting a man in Billings who let me hang around his antiques shop for hours and look at old highway maps. A woman phoned and said her husband had died and she wanted to sell some bowls. We climbed into his El Camino and drove around until we found her sitting in a lawn chair outside a trailer. She couldn't hear, and she had lumbago and a small dog that began biting my ankle. "I want to get on with my life," she yelled, and apparently she meant without any bowls. "Puff!" she called, but the dog didn't go to her, and I had to walk dragging him by his mouth. She let us go inside the trailer, and it was stuffed full of old newspapers with just a skinny path you could walk through. This is what it gets like, I thought, when you can't let go.

It was obvious that the woman was trying to turn over a new leaf, so we bought all her bowls. I got a gigantic stoneware one with a flat bottom, like you'd use if you were making bread for the army, and I knew I would have to change my whole life to have a use for this bowl.

She sold me a box of old Ball jars for three dollars, and there were dead bees inside them. I dragged Puff toward the El Camino. "Do you still can?" I asked.

She shook her head. "My trains of thought don't run that far anymore," she said.

I had started a lot of new collections to get my mind off my problems. I now had a whole room-ful of moody oil paintings of flowers and another room filled with hand-tinted photographs of wa-terfalls with the colors too bright. In the kitchen, there wasn't any more room for all the dishes from the thirties and forties, all the Russell Wright and the Red Wing. I only had one bed, but now I had dozens of worn-out flannel camp blankets, even one covered in race cars. I had a million picnic bas-kets, though I hadn't gone on a picnic in years, and to accessorize them, I bought stacks of floral table-cloths from the forties. I had enough glasses with flower or dog decals to serve drinks for the army I was expecting when I learned to bake bread. On my desk, there were a hundred little plastic Chris Craft inboard boats, and out in the yard, those handmade wooden birds were on sticks all over the garden. This was just the tip of the iceberg of stuff I'd found. "You're like Martha Stewart on crack," my neighbor shouted as I stuck another cardinal in with the daisies.

Back in the guy's shop, I was looking at an old black-and-white postcard of a rock cliff. The caption said, "The Cow in a Milk Bottle," and I couldn't, even squinting, get either the cow or the milk bottle. The guy in the store, to get my attention, was holding up a camp blanket that was covered in spaceships going around Jupiters. He was saying, "All the stuff is just yours for the time you've got it. It's not yours forever. You enjoy it, and then you hope that the next person appreciates it just as much." I suddenly saw that this philosophy also ought to apply to relationships, and when I looked down, the cow was stuck in a big milk bottle.

Because red peppers make a sort of zippy new jelly, it's a good one to make if the whole idea of canning makes you feel like your own grandmother. On the other hand, canning, like collecting, can pull you into another time, which can be

a relief if your own history is the thing you most
want to get away from.

HALF-PINT JARS

2 ½ RED BELL PEPPERS

3 OR 4 HOT PEPPERS

2 CUPS CIDER VINEGAR

2 TEASPOONS SALT

2 TEASPOONS CHILI POWDER

10 CUPS SUGAR

⅔ CUP LEMON JUICE

1 6-OUNCE BOTTLE LIQUID PECTIN

*1. Wear rubber gloves when you cut open the hot pep-
pers, so you don't hurt your hands. Cut open and throw
out the seeds and the white ribs of the peppers, the hot
ones and the sweet ones. Put all the peppers in a*

blender—*the old models look like skyscrapers*—*and whir it until they're finely chopped up. I bought my blender at a pawnshop in Billings, from a woman named Charlotte who said I looked like a movie star because I was wearing sunglasses indoors. It wasn't a style thing, it was from crying so much, but I'd done that even more when I was with my ex-boyfriend than after he'd left.*

You should end up with about 4 cups of this pepper goo. Wash, then sterilize the jars for 10 minutes in boiling water. Leave them in the hot water till you're ready to use them. Bring enough water to a boil to cover the lids and rings in a small pan and leave them in the water.

2. Put the chopped peppers in a saucepan and bring to a boil. Boil for 10 minutes, stirring occasionally. Add the sugar and lemon juice, the vinegar, chili powder, and salt. Bring this back to a boil.

3. Stir in the pectin and boil for only one minute. Remove the boiling syrup from the heat and skim off any foam with a metal spoon. It'll be like a layer of scum across the top of the syrup, and you have to shake the spoon hard to get it off. Fill the dry, hot jars with the jelly, leaving ¼ inch of headspace.

4. Wipe the jar rims clean with the tip of a towel dipped in the boiling water bath, removing any jelly that's dripped onto the rims or sides. Place the hot lids on the jars and screw the rings on firmly. Process in the boiling water canner for 10 minutes. Stop here. You probably think, in general, you could have done more. It was never about your doing more, it was always about trusting that it was out of your hands. After three or four hours, test for a seal on each jar by poking on the top of the lid.

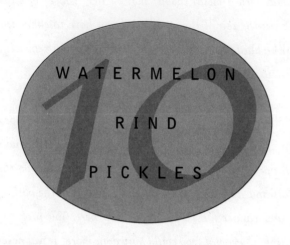

WATERMELON

RIND

PICKLES

I DECIDED I should stop trying to analyze everything. Maybe, I reasoned, I simply needed a change
of scenery, and I left to live for a while on an outer
island in the Bahamas. I helped out as a scuba-
diving instructor at a resort called, ominously,
Small Hope. It shut down for one week and was
taken over by a psychologist who was leading a
workshop, named for himself, called the Wiley

Lab. About forty people came from all over, and most of them were afraid of the water. As part of the course they were taking, they would learn to scuba dive.

The first afternoon, I was standing on the boat, lifting air tanks on board. Nearly everyone was already on the boat, but an older woman in a blue swimsuit dawdled on the dock. "We're ready to go, if you'll climb on," I said. The woman just looked at me.

"I don't have to," she said.

"No, you don't," I said, "but we're all ready to leave."

She bent over so I could read her name tag. It said, "I Don't Have To."

"We all picked names that explain the personal problems we're working on this week," she explained. She climbed on the boat with a middle-aged man whose name tag said, "Castrated."

Every morning, I passed the dining room on my way to the dock, and I could hear them barking and howling inside. Then they'd come out to the dive boat, and they'd have new names on their name tags. The man who had called himself "Castrated" changed his name at one point to "Fraidy Cat."

I had rented my bungalow furnished, and most of the broken furniture on the island seemed to be stored in it. The living room was little, but there were four sofas, one a vinyl paisley in a glittering gold and another a dark brown plaid wool. There was a whole wall of broken dressers in the bedroom, and in one corner, they were two-deep. Except for the one octagon-shaped cottage, where the customs man lived with all his furniture covered in the plastic wrap it came in, all ten little bungalows near mine looked alike. There were palm and hibiscus trees, and it looked like pictures

I've seen of trailer parks in Florida where there's always a big orange sun on a sign over the driveway.

My next-door neighbor was a woman named Cinderella. She had a bumper sticker on her living-room window that said, "Holy Ghost is power!" Through the wall, I could hear the gospel music she played on the stereo. Once when I went over to borrow a mop, she was lying on the sofa, holding a hymn book in one hand and singing "The Old Rugged Cross." She had three young boys who liked to stand on my porch and look in the window at me, like I was Bruce Springsteen.

Another neighbor was a young teacher from Ireland. One day she came over to ask me what I thought of the fact that her students wanted to sing "She'll Be Coming 'Round the Mountain" as the day's hymn. She told me she loved flying, especially the part when the stewardess announces that it's time to put your woolies on. There was also an elderly American who wore a white life preserver around her middle like a doughnut when she went in the water, though it was only about two feet deep. She'd ask me to watch her in the water, and I'd think of the movie about Baby Jane.

I had pushed my good friends away from me and my bad relationship, and this was the first time in years that there were people running around in my life. My favorite was a veterinarian from Guyana. He performed surgery on cats and dogs on my dining-room table. He'd explain everything to me, like I was a medical student, and it was a little romantic. One day, as he anesthetized Scuppy, we sang along with a Luther Vandross record. Then, after surgery, we sat down at the table, with Scuppy lying unconscious between us, without his testicles, and ate watermelon.

At home, I could lock the doors and feel like

I could keep the world out, but on the island, the house was like an oven unless the door was wide open. The things to dread were smaller but they walked right in—the banana spiders, the land crabs, the stinging ants. All in all, I felt safer and I knew it was because I was defenseless.

After a few months, I went back to Montana. Whenever I ate watermelon, I thought of the veterinarian and, occasionally, Scuppy. In canning, there's something a little weird, sort of sickeningly thrifty, about using up the part of the watermelon that's normally left on your plate, but that's the part you need for these pickles.

PINT OR QUART JARS

WATERMELON

PICKLING SALT

FOR THE BRINE:

6 CUPS SUGAR

4 CUPS WATER

2 CUPS VINEGAR

2 TEASPOONS CINNAMON

2 TABLESPOONS ALLSPICE, WHOLE

$1\frac{1}{2}$ TEASPOONS GROUND CLOVES

1 TEASPOON GROUND GINGER

1. Cut off the dark green outer skin as well as all the inner pink meat. Or go around after everyone has eaten and collect all the leftover watermelon rinds. You make the pickles with the pale green rind only. Cut the rind into one-inch cubes. *Let the cubes stand overnight in enough salted water to cover them.*

2. *Sterilize the jars and pour boiling water over the lids and rings and leave them in the water. Mix together all the ingredients for the brine in an enamelware or nonanodized metal saucepan. Heat just to a boil.*

3. *Drain off the salt water, then pack the watermelon cubes into the jars. Pack in as much as you possibly can. Now pour the brine over the rind in the jars, leaving ½ inch of headspace.*

4. *Wipe the jar rims clean with the tip of a towel dipped in the boiling water bath. Place the hot lids on the jars and screw the rings on firmly. Process in the boiling water canner for 20 minutes (add one minute for every 1,000 feet above sea level). Let the pickles ripen for 6 weeks in a cool, dark room, then give them away.*

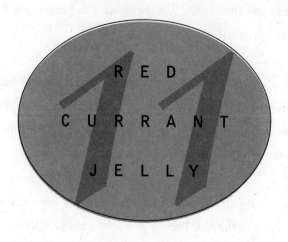

RED CURRANT JELLY

ON A plane, I met a dermatologist who did laser plastic surgery. The doctor thought it would be fun if I saw the process his patients went through. "Look in this mirror," he said, "and tell me what you hate about yourself when you first get up in the morning." I looked hard. "Well, I guess these bags under my eyes, " I said, playing along.

He looked genuinely surprised. He said, "I would have thought you'd say, 'All these deep lines all over my face.'"

Now I hated the way I looked. I was going to Los Angeles, so I went to visit Cara. I told her that I had to lose weight. She rolled her eyes. "You white women are suicidal at the point when a black woman is just starting to think about going on a diet."

She said, "We've got to jack up your joy level," and we got in the car. She explained that we had an appointment to visit a psychic she knew. We met her in a small room, and the woman told me she could see all the people in the spirit world standing around me.

"Your grandmother is putting all sorts of hats on your head," the woman said. "She says you must never let your hair go gray." I couldn't believe I was even getting beauty advice from spirits. "The last man tore your heart out," she continued, "but the next one is coming soon," she said, and she smiled. "He's very bland."

"Blond?" I asked.

She looked into the spirit world and wrinkled her nose. "Bland-looking," she said.

"Well, great," I said when we left.

"Knock it off," Cara said. "I mean, can't you have a higher purpose? Then it doesn't matter who's around you. Be self-fulfilled. You are so desperate to be attached. You don't even know these men, and then you wonder why it turns out awful. It was always awful!"

We drove to a Pic N Save, and we were so engrossed in talk that we just pushed an empty cart around, and pretty soon I noticed a woman with another empty cart was following us, leaning in to hear. "It's your spirit that leads you to the places where the broken hearts are, and you are left with how to survive anyway. That's how you learn to be really happy," Cara was saying. I knew it was the Motown connection that made me willing to listen to her. Black music had led me to my whole so-called career, and that made me a pushover when black people talked to me about other things. I felt they had some secret, and no matter how weird the conversations got—I'd grown up in a house where you only said "Christ" if you spilled something—I hung in, wanting to get the secret myself.

We started wheeling further, and the woman behind us just left her cart and joined us. "You're just a train on a track," Cara said, now talking more to the stranger than to me. "The train picks people up and passes people by. Sometimes there's a little car riding by your side, and then maybe it goes off, and maybe it comes back. You are not in control of who comes and rides by your side for those times." The stranger nodded.

"Everything is a piece in the puzzle, a clue to something you'll understand only if you stay on the track," Cara said, walking off, arms locked, with the stranger. It wasn't the first or the last time that I watched two black women almost instantly treat each other like sisters. I felt chastened. I didn't even treat my own sister like my sister.

Before I left Los Angeles, I was walking back from a 7-Eleven one day, when I saw a really big man in a nice suit, standing up ahead with his luggage, the trunk open on his Rolls-Royce. He had a pressed white shirt on a hanger in one hand, and he was standing like he was frozen, not sure about how to fit everything in the trunk. It was a long walk up the street, and he didn't move the whole time. When I got up beside the car, I walked over and asked if I could help. It was Muhammad Ali. He didn't answer, so I just put the suitcases in the trunk. A woman came running toward us from an apartment building, and he went to her. I had met a lot of famous people for my work, but I was over-whelmed by Ali, by the thoughts afterward about the fights you can win and the fights you can't win. If there was one thing that had pushed me to get over what had happened, it was when the thought that life is short crashed through.

When I got back home, I tried to remember what Cara had said, and I wrote down some notes so I could try to figure it out. You can see from the red spots all over the page that I was also making currant jelly. Red currants are easy to come by in the summer, and they jell easily. If you're sick of things not turning out the way you wanted, this is just what the doctor ordered. Okay, he ordered Prozac, but this is infallible.

HALF-PINT JARS

CURRANTS (ABOUT 5 POUNDS)

SUGAR

STICK CINNAMON

WHOLE CLOVES

1. Wash the currants gently in cold water and remove any stalks or leaves, but you don't have to remove all the tiny stems. Mash slightly to start the juice, then add just a little water—no more than half a cup. Cook slowly for about 10 minutes, until the currants look white. Drain in a wet jelly bag for at least six hours or overnight. Don't squeeze the jelly bag to extract the juice. Don't force things.

2. Sterilize the jars for 10 minutes in boiling water.
    Years before, I had met Don King at a party in a museum for Michael Jackson. He had just moved from box-

ing to music promoting, and I don't think he had a total grip on the big picture. I'd barely written anything then, but he dragged Michael Jackson up to me and referred to me, twice, and loudly, as "the world-famous. . . ." As he worked the room, I could hear him calling almost everybody "world-famous," and I bet that's why he's so popular.

It was the exact reverse of something I'd done. While I was going to college, I got a job working in a bar in Chicago for Joe Pepitone, who had opened a place called, in an old-fashioned, swinging way, Joe Pepitone's Thing. One night, I was bartending when I gave an old guy the bill for his beer. He handed it back and said, "I'm Yogi Berra." I said, "So?" blankly, and it is hard to imagine that I was ever that young. We had to wear little Cubs uniforms to work. When I walked back to my car late at night, men thought I was a streetwalker with a sales gimmick, and I was constantly asked to hold their bats.

Pour boiling water over the lids and rings and leave them in the water at least 3 minutes or until you're ready to use them.

3. *Measure the juice, and put it in a stainless steel or enamelware pan, something with a big, flat bottom. Work with no more than four cups of juice at a time. You can eliminate the next step with the spices if you want to make just plain currant jelly. Tie the spices in cheesecloth and boil with the extracted juice for 10 minutes. Remove the bag of spices. If you are using black or white currants, or wild gooseberries, in this recipe, you have to add 2 tablespoons of fresh lemon juice with the sugar.*

Add ¾ cup of sugar for every cup of juice, stirring until all the sugar is dissolved. Boil rapidly to the jelly stage. Carefully spoon off the scum that forms on the surface of the syrup. There is usually quite a lot of scum, and you can hurl it onto a plate as you go along, then throw it away afterward. Begin to test whether it's done after about 10 minutes. Use the spoon, or sheeting, test. Review the whole method in the earlier crab-apple recipe if you need to, but don't use that as an excuse to drag yourself back into the past. You didn't do anything wrong.

4.   *Remove the boiling syrup from the heat and skim off*
any more of the foam—the scum, not the little boiling
bubbles. This step ought to reassure you that your judg-
ment is good, no matter what has happened: you can tell
scum from bubbles. Fill the dry, hot jars with the jelly.
You don't want to put the hot syrup into cold jars: you
know what a shock like that can do. Leave ¼ inch of head-
space. Wipe the jar rims clean with the tip of a towel
dipped in the boiling water bath. Process in the boiling
water canner for 10 minutes, then give the jelly away.

12

SPICY MARINATED MUSHROOMS

I HAD hiked and hoped for grizzly bears. I had kayaked because it seemed like it would be easy to hit your head and drown. I had rollerskated on the runway of the local airport, and I had used my headphones, in the hopes that I would miss the sound of an approaching plane. When I didn't think I could go on living, I had spent more and more time outside doing new things, and I wondered why it had taken a disaster. I learned that nobody is wondering why you don't have a husband and family or something better to do than ride a bike around in a forest. And out in the trees, whatever happened to you is insignificant. Your perspective gets adjusted without a lot of mental strain.

Late one afternoon when the sky was pink, I decided to dust off my ice skates, and I ran over to the pond in the middle of town. I was skating along when a man skated up beside me. He talked about ice crystals and how they form downward and why the pond is frozen solid. I didn't mind the company, but all of a sudden I could tell he was about to skate off. "Well, I think you're pretty," he said, "but I know you're just thinking, 'There goes the smarty pants of ice.'"

I hadn't thought that at all, but I did understand that you could come to believe that your strengths were your weaknesses. The whole time I was in high school, I had to take home economics. I learned to sew, to repair things, to cook, and to can. Then I forced myself to use none of this knowledge, until my depression drove me to jelly. I had stayed in the closet about all those domestic things, like growing up in Wisconsin was something you could grow out of, but now a new mountain-biking trail had opened near my mother's hometown, which wasn't far from mine, and I felt compelled to drive back there.

In the town where my mother grew up, they had what they called the Musky Festival, and we used to have to go to it. What made it different from my own town's fair, which was called Wannigan Days, or even the nearby Rutabaga Festival, were two things: one was a contest to catch the biggest muskelunge, and the other was when a plane flew overhead and dropped Ping-Pong balls on everybody. There were numbers written on the balls that corresponded to prizes, and only one ball had the number for the grand prize, which was a hundred dollars. That was the thing about growing up in northern Wisconsin: the best you could hope for was not very good.

I walked around the town now, and the things that had always depressed me, like the display of the World Record Muskelunge, didn't seem that pathetic. It was a big fish. On the back roads, I drove past all those lake cottages named "The Dun Vonderin," and I didn't feel personally embarrassed anymore. Then, somehow, I wound up out at the Turk's Supper Club. When I was a kid, I knew from TV that nobody in New York City ever talked about "supper clubs," and I used to die inside that that's what my father called our restaurant. I always hoped that nobody would ask me who belonged to it. Nothing at Turk's had changed, and I settled into a booth and realized that I really felt comfortable in the middle of nowhere, where I was from. It had been the fountain of all this sorrow, and it wasn't worth it.

I tried to drive the whole rest of the way back to my house without stopping. It seemed to be a lot farther than the signs said it was, like you really should multiply the miles in North Dakota by something, like figuring a dog's age. But suddenly there was a storm, the heavens hurling snow cones at the windshield, and I pulled into the town of Medora.

The town was dead, out of season, and the motel man opened a freezing room so I could stay overnight. I walked through town, and that's when I saw Elvis. He was unmistakable, mostly because he had on one of his white jumpsuits, with the big gold belt. He ducked into a dance hall in town. "Elvis is here," I told the man at the motel when I got back. "Oh, he's the Sioux Falls Elvis," the guy said.

The next morning, I stopped to see Teddy Roosevelt's tiny cabin on the outskirts of town.

He'd come here to deal with his despair after his wife and his mother died just hours apart. It's when he was in North Dakota that he fell in love with the West and made himself strong enough to start over again. You couldn't help but see, considering the whole story, how depression has a function, that it's a way to figure out what you need to do in your life and that it drives you to new places where you suddenly bump into Elvis. In the gift shop, I opened up a book to a line Roosevelt had written about the same thing: "Black care rarely sits behind a rider whose pace is fast enough."

When I got back home, I walked over to the grocery store. Mushrooms are always available at the store, so it doesn't need to be harvest season to make pickled mushrooms.

Years ago I had interviewed Brigitte Nielsen, a Danish actress who had wrangled a marriage to Sylvester Stallone. We were talking about the pressures of fame, and she said she and her husband were followed everywhere. I asked her, "Can you do normal things, like go to the grocery store?" She said, very dramatically, "I do not want to go to the grocery store."

HALF-PINT JARS

SMALL WHOLE MUSHROOMS, VERY FRESH,
WITH CAPS ABOUT AN INCH IN DIAMETER

BOTTLED LEMON JUICE

FOR THE BRINE:

2½ CUPS DISTILLED WHITE, CIDER, OR AN
HERB-FLAVORED VINEGAR (5% ACIDITY)

2 CUPS OLIVE OIL

1 TABLESPOON OREGANO

1 TABLESPOON BASIL

1 TABLESPOON PICKLING SALT

½ CUP CHOPPED ONIONS

FOR ADDING TO THE JARS:

GARLIC CLOVES

BLACK PEPPERCORNS

1. Wash the mushrooms, or just wipe the dirt off with a wet paper towel. Cut the stem to just below the cap. Cover the mushrooms in a saucepan with water and add some lemon juice, about ½ cup for every quart of water. Bring to a boil and simmer for 5 minutes, then drain. This makes the mushrooms shrivel up some so that when you put them in the jars, they stay tightly packed. Otherwise, it would look like you gave up before you finished filling the jars.

2. Wash, then boil the jars for 10 minutes. Use pretty little jars, if you can. This is supposed to be sort of fancy.

Leave them in the hot water till you're ready to use them. Pour boiling water over the lids and rings and leave them in the water until you're ready to use them, at least 3 minutes.

I got the assignment to talk to the then Mrs. Stallone from Interview, *which was owned at the time by Andy Warhol. I was in an editor's office when he walked in. He asked me what I was going to ask her, and I told him that I wanted to talk to her about luck and fate, about which of those had accounted for her sudden romantic windfall. He looked very disappointed. He said, "Can't you just ask her what Sylvester is like in bed?" Now I know, of course, that it isn't so important to know whether luck or fate brings you something, but whether you can let go of it.*

3. Mix the vinegar, olive oil, oregano, basil, pickling salt (you can't substitute table salt), and onions in a stainless steel or enamelware saucepan. Heat, stirring occasionally, to boiling.

4. Place half a garlic clove and some peppercorns in each half-pint jar. Fill the jars with the mushrooms. I mean, you have to really pack them in, like when you have to sit on the suitcase. Then pour in the hot oil-and-vinegar solution, leaving ½ inch of headspace.

5. Wipe the jar rims clean with the tip of a towel dipped in the clean hot water that the jars were boiled in. Place the hot lids on the jars and screw the rings on firmly. Process in the boiling water canner for 20 minutes. Don't tighten the screw bands after boiling the jars, or you'll have to get a really strong new boyfriend before you can eat any mushrooms. Let ripen for at least 4 weeks.

BLUEBERRY BUTTER

I KNEW I had turned a corner when I no longer wondered why my ex-boyfriend had left, but why it hadn't ended sooner. Around this time, I noticed my friends were calling in tears—Larry or Roger had thrown skis or a barbecue grill at them, and they were devastated. It was over, they'd say, until the end of the conversation, when they'd pulled themselves together. One day I was with a friend at her boyfriend's apartment when he described his holiday plans, which didn't include her. She was sobbing when we left. "It's not what I'm looking for," she said, "to spend holidays by myself. It's finished." We only walked a couple of blocks, then she pointed at some expensive drinking glasses in a store window. "Do you think he'd like those?" she said, going for her purse.

That's why I decided to go to the murder trial of Clara Hess, back in Montana. She'd managed to end her relationship. I took a seat in a row with some elderly women. I thought maybe they were Clara's bridge club. "We're all here from the battered women's shelter," a woman whispered to me. Clara herself was a tiny grandmother. She'd poisoned her husband after dinner one night and then told everyone he was on a fishing trip.

Bill was not catching any trout. A next-door neighbor, hired by Clara, had unknowingly buried him. He had a company with the slogan, "Have

Gravel, Will Travel," that I'd seen on a billboard when I was driving around. It turns out that you're not asked very many questions when you order a load of gravel big enough to fill a man-sized hole.

The more Clara talked, I saw that even she hadn't been able to end her relationship. All her husband ever did was yell at her, and she'd married him anyway—twice. She couldn't recall the day that her husband had gone into the root cellar that last time or what had finally gotten to her, but she remembered every dessert she'd ever served. I suppose she focused on the only thing that she could completely control. As the prosecutor attempted to lead her to Bill's last breath, Clara was sorting out whether they'd just eaten tapioca or cling peaches.

I felt relieved, even as Clara went to the slammer. If everything had worked out the way I'd wanted it to, I would've ended up like Clara, dreaming about arsenic pie.

I bought a buff-colored 1964 Chevy convertible and took it with the top down in a pointless circle around the state, enjoying how good it felt not to have anybody yelling at me or swatting me on the leg while I was driving, like Clara said Bill always did. I stopped one afternoon at a bar in a place known as the Valley of the Eagles. The town, Ringling, is famous for once having been the winter home of the Ringling Brothers and Barnum & Bailey Circus. The circus animals arrived by the trainload every year to have a few months' rest. The bartender was telling me about the town, or what little was left of it besides the bar. "Our bank collapsed," he said.

"Well, banks everywhere collapsed this year," I said, trying to be reassuring that this little town was not alone in its economic problems.

He looked confused. "I mean it literally fell down," he said.

I stopped next in a town called Boulder, just

to see what it meant when it said "health mine" on a sign near the town. At the Lone Tree Health Mine, the owner told me that the radon gas in his abandoned mine could cure just about everything. It was the good kind of radon, he explained, not the bad kind that you have in your basement. He gave me a free hour and a big glass of radioactive water to drink while I sat in a plastic chair by my-self in an underground tunnel. Normally, he said, the place was full of elderly people from all over the world, who played Yahtzee and wrote com-ments in the guest book. "My husband's arthritic thumbs were moving without that clicking noise," a woman wrote. "I'm breathing more easily now that my boyfriend's gone," I added at the end.

Up near Glacier Park, I bought blueberries at a roadside stand. Once, I went to an astrologer who told me that you can't let anyone yell at you. "Your throat chakra is blocked," she said gravely. "You need more blue food." I had to admit that I didn't feel a need to make anything out of the berries when I got home.

---

4 CUPS BLUEBERRIES

6 APPLES, PEELED AND CHOPPED (4 CUPS)

2 CUPS WHITE SUGAR

1 CUP LIGHT BROWN SUGAR

1 TEASPOON GROUND CINNAMON

¼ TEASPOON GROUND ALLSPICE

¼ TEASPOON GROUND NUTMEG

1. *Combine everything in a saucepan and cook over low heat, dissolving the sugar while stirring. If you're really depressed, just the fact that the sugar actually disappears into the fruit seems like a major win. So when it boils like it's supposed to, and all you've done is turn up the heat, which is the next step, you're almost having a good day.*

Now simmer uncovered for about 45 minutes, stirring more near the end of the time so stuff doesn't burn on the bottom and wreck how well things are going. After all, the small things add up. I passed through Drummond, Idaho, once, and they have a big sign in the middle of town. It lists the population, the altitude, the average temperature, and the year it was founded. And then at the bottom, it says, "Total——"and all those numbers are added together. It's a big number, for such a small town.

2. *While the fruit's simmering, sterilize the jars and lids and rings and leave them in hot water.*

3. *Test for doneness of the fruit butter by putting a dab on a cold plate: if no ring of liquid seeps out, it's done. Another test: does it look like it would stick to your toast? Pour the butter into the jars, filling to within ¼ inch of the rims. Wipe the rims with a clean damp cloth and seal the jars with the lids. Process for 10 minutes.*

DILL

GREEN

TOMATO

PICKLES

14

THERE WERE two things I wanted to do in India: one was to go to see the nadi reader, a man who can read your past and future off ancient palm leaves, and the other was to see Sai Baba, a guru with a big Afro. I'd heard that people's lives turned around after they saw him. They were saying it was like Jesus himself was walking around India. It was far, but not too far if you could jump-start a happy new life. The fallback plan was that I'd read that Mother Teresa had started a new project there called, "A Home for the Bewildered."

In the south, near Bangalore, I met up with a German named Frank. We were standing outside a temple near a statue of what looked like a giant pirate when a little girl in a yellow sari came up to us. She was named after some god, and so was her sister, and by the time she'd tried to explain just the basics of Hinduism, I knew I was coming too late to the party.

Inside the temple, people were carrying coconuts and bananas and handing them to priests swathed in white, who carried the fruit deep into a silver chamber, where they fed it to monkeys. Then a priest came out of the monkey room and held a big offering plate out to me. "Take this," he whispered, pressing a banana into my hands.

Frank and I slipped off through a passageway around the side of the temple. I couldn't figure out

what to do with the banana. "Maybe I was supposed to pass it along," I said. Frank was baffled.
He had yellow and red smudges on his forehead
that a priest had wiped on him with his thumb. Suddenly, a very handsome man in a gold toga was in
front of us. He smiled broadly. I figured he was the
top priest.

I hoped that he'd say something that would
clear up all the confusion. "Excuse me," I said, "but
what am I supposed to do with the banana?"

He looked at me kind of pathetically and said,
"Eat it?"

I pinned my hopes on Sai Baba. I took a long
bus trip, and at four in the morning, I lined up with
a thousand women outside an enormous baby-pink
temple. The men were somewhere on the other
side. Almost everybody had on white cotton paja-
mas. We sat on a cement walkway for hours, then
we were led into the temple, where we sat on the
floor for a couple more hours, waiting silently. I

was surrounded by people in blue kerchiefs that said "Argentina" or "Ivory Coast" or other places around the world. Finally some music that sounded like water started to play on the loudspeakers, and a tiny man in a geranium-colored robe came in, walking really, really slowly. He looked like he could be the Jacksons' grandfather.

He was swirling his hand around in the air, almost like he was signaling everybody to stand up, but nobody did. He walked around the whole temple, just motioning with his hand, and then he was gone and the music stopped. Everyone got up to go home.

I was incredulous. "Is that it?" I whispered to a woman whose kerchief said, "Croatia." She nodded. "Doesn't he ever say anything?" I asked her. She shook her head.

"When he speaks to you," she whispered back, "it's not going to be that way." I rolled my eyes. "You'll see," she said, "you'll be happier when you get home." Unless I had to wait outside on my own sidewalk for four hours, I was sure she was right.

I traveled back across the country on the bus and went to see the palm-leaf reader, hoping his communication would be out loud. He wore a golf shirt and a white cloth tied like a diaper. He took a stack of dried old leaves out of a padlocked room. There was faint writing on them in Sanskrit. He turned them over, one by one, and named the year my father had died, the year I'd moved to New York, and other details of my life. He even said that I'd written about music. He was right about everything. Then he said he had to tell me about my past lives, and happily, I hadn't been Joan of Arc or Amelia Earhart, like most of the people I knew. He said, "All of this, the people leaving you, had to happen so you could see that you are never really alone. You see now that all of those people can go, and you'll be fine. You need to know you're not a small person who's afraid someone will leave you—all these lives you've had, all these lifetimes to meet up with people again and again.

"And now all your loneliness is in the past," he said, "and next year, you will marry a man not from Canada or America. A European man."

He stopped reading the leaf and looked over at me. "You happy?" he asked. I pictured those Italian men in their Speedos, but I said it was okay, I just hoped my husband spoke English. I already knew he was going to be bland. "Well," he said brightly, "maybe he's from England." I was thinking that he should know, when he said, in a different, almost jolly voice, "Your visit made Sai Baba very, very happy!" I fell back into the chair. Then he hurried out of the room with his leaves.

I ran after him. "Excuse me," I said, "but how did you know about Sai Baba?"

He looked at me blankly. "What are you talking about?" he asked.

"The last thing you said . . . ," I said, slowly,

hoping I could jar his short-term memory. He closed his eyes, like he was thinking. "You said my visit made Sai Baba very happy," I said, finally.

He looked completely stumped. "Sorry," he said. "Not me. Maybe Sai Baba was talking to you?" I glared at him. "Why do you act like something's gone wrong? Why not just accept and move on, instead of stop and try to figure out?" he asked. "Your visit made Sai Baba happy. Maybe there's nothing else to know about that." And then he shuffled away in his rubber thongs.

At the Dum Dum Airport in Calcutta, I looked up to see the back of my cab as it pulled away. Across the trunk, in yellow paint, it said, "Life is play, world is stage, people are actors, God is director."

I'd never been so happy to find my way home. I had a vegetable garden all in pots, so that when things died, I could just shove the pots into the garage. There were a million little tomatoes still hanging on, but they were all green. When there's a frost coming, you just have to pick them and use them up all at once. I stood out by the tomatoes and thought about the fact that it had simply never occurred to me not to look for my fault in whatever happened, not to figure out how I'd personally made everything go haywire. I'd gone halfway around the world to learn to say, "Maybe there's nothing more to know about that," and just move ahead, which is the only way you can go in those rubber thongs, anyway.

QUART OR PINT JARS

GREEN TOMATOES

STALK OF CELERY

SWEET GREEN PEPPERS

GARLIC CLOVES

FRESH DILL WEED (YOU WON'T BE MAKING
ANYTHING WITH GREEN TOMATOES AT A TIME
WHEN YOU WON'T ALSO HAVE FRESH DILL
AVAILABLE)

FOR THE BRINE:

2 QUARTS WATER

1 QUART DISTILLED WHITE VINEGAR (5%
ACIDITY)

1 CUP PICKLING SALT

1. Slice the tomatoes about ¼ inch thick. Pack them into clean, sterilized jars. To each quart jar, add some dill weed and a clove of garlic, then put a 4-inch stalk of celery down a side of the jar and slide down the other sides some slices of green pepper. Make it look organized and pretty.

2. Put the lids and the rings in another small saucepan, cover them with water, and bring it just to a boil. Turn

off the heat, and leave them in the water until you're ready to use them.

Make the brine by combining the water, vinegar, and salt and boiling in a stainless steel or enamelware saucepan for 5 minutes. Use a big-mouthed funnel, and pour the brine over the pickles in the jars, leaving ½ inch of headspace. If there are air bubbles in the mix, poke a long wooden spoon handle or a chopstick down the side of the jar until you release them.

3. Wipe the jar rims clean with the tip of a towel dipped in the boiling water bath. Place the hot lids on the jars and screw the rings on firmly. Process in the boiling water canner for 20 minutes. Let the pickles ripen for 6 weeks, and then give a jar to somebody.

CINNAMON PRUNE MARMALADE

I DECIDED to enter some of the contests at the local county fair. In the horticulture competition, there was a category called, "Wild and Free," that stipulated it had to be "an arrangement of flowers and animals" and another called, "Glad You Came," that had to be gladiolas. I entered one called, "Trail of the Lonesome Pine." The note on the vase said

I was disqualified. "You were supposed to use rocks," somebody had written.

I also entered some jellies and jams. When I went to see if I'd won, I met a woman who said she'd entered thirty-two different kinds of canned goods. "My husband died this year," she said, but it went without saying. I could tell by the flowers she was holding that she had also entered "Glad You Came."

I won the second-place ribbon for my plum jam, though there were only two entries. The other was from a twelve-year-old. I made two dollars.

I was happy again. I didn't really have to look for answers farther than my own kitchen. I had gone a really long way to get back home.

"You know, it was really meaningless to go through all that grief," Cara said to me, when I called to tell her what I'd won. "If you just keep living, it all makes sense. It's like the marchers with the flags on the football field," she said. "They're directed to take two steps to the left, then ten steps forward, and two to the right. It doesn't seem like it could possibly be right. It seems like a big mess. It feels meaningless. But up in the stands, finally, from a distance, they're making something really beautiful. You just have to trust the directions and not worry that it's not working out. There's a pattern there."

I hung up when the mailman came to the door with a small package. The return address was the mental hospital's. I couldn't imagine what the boy could send. I opened the box and inside were two jars: he had been making jelly. "I'm not so depressed anymore," he wrote.

Not long after that, I went back to New York, and I carried the pages of a novel written by a man I'd never met. It was good, though, and because I'd given up on my own true-crime book, I decided I would try to help this man find a way to publish his book. I went to a meeting at a big publishing company, and the editor looked unhappy. He didn't really like the novel, he said, and then he added that things weren't going well at home. So maybe I wasn't here about work at all, I thought. He told me about his life.

"You should try making jelly," I said. I told him about how canning had helped me get through the worst times, skipping right through feel, felt, and found. I noticed a light go on in his eyes. Then suddenly I thought I could see, for the first time in a really long while, what the pattern was out on the field.

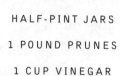

HALF-PINT JARS

1 POUND PRUNES

1 CUP VINEGAR

BLUE JELLY

1 ½ CUPS SUGAR

½ TEASPOON GROUND CLOVES

½ TEASPOON GROUND CINNAMON

1. *First you have to buy the prunes, and you have to stand there in the store while the check-out person looks at you to see if you appear constipated. You can't care what anyone else thinks. Cover the prunes with water, then let simmer for an hour.*

Drain, saving the liquid, and remove the pits from the prunes and cut them into small pieces.

2. *Wash, then sterilize the jars for 10 minutes in boiling water. Leave them in the hot water till you're ready to use them. In a separate pan, bring water to a boil over the lids and rings and leave them in the hot water, too. You know all this, but there are lots of things you need to be told over and over, like, especially, nothing is ever*

taken from you without its being replaced by something better.

3. Return the cut-up prunes to the heat with the liquid you simmered them in, and add the vinegar, sugar, and spices. Simmer until thick, like 45 minutes or an hour.

4. Pour into sterilized jars, leaving ¼ inch of headspace. Wipe the jar rims clean with the tip of a towel dipped in the boiling water bath. Place hot lids on jars and screw rings on firmly. Process in the boiling water canner for 10 minutes.

One day, while I was waiting out the time while the jars boiled, a magazine arrived with an article by my exboyfriend that included, in an emotional history of himself, a paragraph about our relationship. He had condensed, I guess for storytelling purposes, the years we were together to a casual summer fling. Finally, I understood why he always used to say, "The pen is not mightier than the sword, it is the sword."

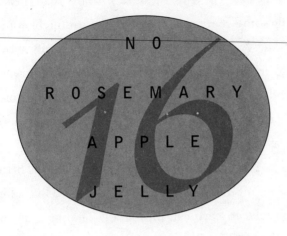

16

NO ROSEMARY APPLE JELLY

EVERY TRIP had held an element of disaster, every new adventure had had a point where it looked meaningless, and every person I met seemed a little strange. But it had all added up to something, and I began to see that it was while I was canning that the addition took place. The point could not be the canning itself, or that I was supposed to hang out forever in my own kitchen. After every batch of jelly, I was back on the road, heading somewhere new, wondering what might come along. And after every road trip, I was back shoving my fingers into the ground and harvesting what had ripened while I was away. It balanced out. There was a lot to collect out in the world and there was a lot to preserve when I got home.

I had to admit that I'd been handed little pieces of the puzzle by people it seemed like a big mistake to have run into at all. The guru in the desert had made me see that you can think you're going somewhere for one reason and wind up finding you're there for something entirely different; the editor, a woman of steel, had taught me that crying may be counterproductive; the country singer had shown me what it looked like to have some faith in yourself. There was some little piece of the puzzle that I had been able to add every time I went outside. These little adventures by myself would be enough.

Then, one night, my phone rang. A friend of mine asked me to come to a restaurant for dinner. He was with another guy, he said, and he wanted me to join them. I couldn't have been less interested. I was just starting to make some rosemary apple jelly. I told him that I couldn't come, and I went down to the basement to get some jars. I looked at a big shelf that was covered with old turquoise Ball jars. There seemed to be millions of them. There was an endless supply, for whenever I needed them, and I knew I didn't really need them now.

I ran up the stairs and grabbed my jacket, then went running in the snow to the restaurant. If I had learned anything, it was that making jelly was something to do when I wasn't out having a life. But it was the getting outside, not the jelly, that had made me happy again.

I got to the restaurant and my heart sank. Maybe they'd gone somewhere else. I stood in the doorway, by myself. Then finally I saw my friend waving from across the room. "I changed my mind," I said, and I looked at the man with him at the table. And there it was, suddenly and quickly, out of nowhere, that feeling I'd almost forgotten, when someone's heart opens to let you in. I knew that I wouldn't be canning again for a while, but I had absorbed in every cell the lesson of jelly: if you are patient enough, it always turns out.

APPENDIX

Better than Botulism:
A few things you need to know about
canning

A Few Points About
Canning, and the
Gear You Need

I nod off whenever I have to read about the point of canning. About botulism. About which fruits have lots of natural pectin. In a nutshell, you go through all the steps described in the recipes, sterilizing everything, because you don't really want to die, no matter how crummy you feel today.

You might want to know that it's harder to make jelly than it is to make jam; there are more steps to jelly. The difference is that jams and fruit butters are thick and have chunks or a purée of fruit in them and are less solid than jellies. Jellies are just the juice, jelled. For jelly, you go along like you're making jam, then you hang the fruit up in a jelly bag and drain off the juice. Then you boil that up with sugar. Jelly is supposed to have a very specific, wiggly-but-firm consistency; jam can be a little firmer or a little looser and no one cares.

Marmalades are more like jellies with peel or tiny pieces of fruit in them. Preserves are whole fruit or big pieces in a slightly jelled syrup. Pickles are a whole other category, and there are dill or sweet varieties.

All of these things require that after you have the food all prepared and sealed in the jars, you have to boil them in a canner—the whole jar set in a bath, a big pot of boiling water—for a given amount of time.

A few months ago, I couldn't stand to shop because every time I would see those bags of Caesar salad, a reminder of picnics with the man I loved, I would cry on the produce. If you cannot fathom that you could get your act together enough to go buy fruit or anything else, take it one step at a time.

Until you feel like going out and rounding up the special gadgets made just for canning, you can improvise with things you already have in the kitchen. First set your sights, modestly, on getting some jars. When you are better, you can collect antique blue ones and old jelly jars, but that can wait.

You need a big kettle that you can boil water in and some sort of rack that will hold the jars off the bottom. A "boiling water canner" with a wire tray to hold the jars is ideal, and you can get one at a yard sale or at the Wal-Mart, whichever brings up fewer memories of your previous life. You also need a thing that pulls the hot jars from the water, but in a pinch, you can use tongs.

You can also buy a thing that looks like a wide-mouthed funnel, which keeps the jelly from slurping down the sides when you ladle it into the jars.

I would advise you to buy this one; there are always a million of them in junk shops. In fact, junk shops usually have a lot of used canning tools, because nobody cans anymore, or so they say. But you don't even really need this funnel; you can always just spoon the jelly into the jars and wipe off whatever drips.

If you feel up to buying everything, here's your shopping list:

- Jelly bag
- Pan big enough to boil large amounts of fruit and sugar, with enough room for it to boil and foam up without getting over the top of the pan, and broad enough on the bottom so the excess liquid evaporates off quickly
- Candy thermometer, if you want to test by temperature, though this actually never works for me

- Wide-mouthed funnel with handle
- Large boiler for sterilizing and processing the glass jars, with a rack to keep the jars a half-inch off the bottom
- Jars and lids and screw bands
- Tongs to lift the jars out of the water
- Tray to hold the jars, before and after you fill them
- New dress

Real Canning Advice

Use new sealing lids. You can reuse jars and rings but not the flat metal lid. If you use jars that have a glass lid attached with wire, you have to use new rubber rings each time. You also need to use new rubber rings if you're using old zinc caps on the jars.

Jars and lids that aren't made for canning, like empty mayonnaise jars, might not withstand the heat.

Don't use jars that have nicks or cracks or rough edges on the rims. Don't use rusty screw bands.

On canning in general:

Leave the amount of "headspace," the space between the top of the food and the jar lid, that is in-
dicated in the recipe. If you don't, and you pack the
food in too tightly, it might turn out under-
processed and spoil. Sometimes when you overfill
the jars, some of the liquid leaks out while you're
boiling the filled jars in the canner. It's really gross
when this happens, but you can't undo the seal and
add more liquid. You have to let it be.

You have to add 1 minute to the time the jars are
being processed in the boiling water for every
1,000 feet you are above sea level. That's because
the boiling point of water decreases with altitude.
So it takes longer to make the food safe from mi-
croorganisms, which is the whole point of the
boiling-water bath.

When you first pull the empty sterilized jars from the pot, put them upside down on a pad of clean towels to drain off the excess water. After you've filled them, don't put the hot jars on a cold surface. The shock could break them. You know how that feels.

Don't can, which is to say, "process the jars after they're full of food," in the oven, in the microwave, in a steamer, or in the dishwasher. Or up in the attic, no matter how hot you think it feels up there.

On jelly & jam:

It's best to use underripe fruit, and it should be freshly picked. Fruit has to have two things in the right proportion to be converted to jelly—pectin and acid—and both decrease as fruit ripens. Because overripe fruit has less pectin, the jelly might not get hard enough, no matter how long you boil it. You can mix it up a little, using underripe fruit to get the pectin, and ripe fruit for full flavor and color. Some fruits—very sweet ones, like bananas and peaches—don't have enough acid, so you add lemon juice; some don't have enough pectin, so you use commercial pectin extract.

For the record, the fruits that have enough natural pectin are apples, blackberries, crab apples, cranberries, currants, gooseberries, grapes, plums, quinces, and raspberries. The idea with preserves is that the fruit should hold its shape and color, and cherries, peaches, pears, plums, quinces, strawberries, tomatoes, and figs are good for this. For jam, you want well-ripened and soft-fleshed fruits like apricots, peaches, and plums.

Commercial pectin can allow you to make more jelly from a small amount of fruit. However, it requires much more sugar.

Cut out any bruises or blemishes on the fruit, and make sure you clean the fruits or vegetables, draining the water off. You don't have to core the apples, and you can leave the skins on them, as well as on grapes, plums, and quinces. You have to take the caps and stems off most berries, though you can leave the tiny stems on currants.

It's better to work with smaller quantities of food, like no more than eight cups of juice, six quarts of berries, or eight pounds of apples. By the way, about two pounds of fruit equals a pint of juice, and a pint of juice with an equal amount of sugar, which is usually what it takes, equals 1½ pints of jelly. Don't double the quantity of a jam or jelly recipe. If there's too much food, it can be hard to figure out the jelling time.

If the recipe says to add just a little water, don't add too much. The idea is that you have to cook the fruit to extract the pectin, which makes the jelly harden; because you don't want the fruit to stick to the bottom of the pan, you add water, but then you have to cook off any added water so that you have enough pectin for the amount of fruit. It's kind of like chemistry class. After you add the sugar, you have to make sure you boil it just until it's jelly. Overcooking may destroy so much pectin that you get a gummy mass, or what I call the jujube state, instead of jelly.

Remember that the jelling point, if you're testing with a candy thermometer, is 8 degrees higher than the boiling point of water, wherever you are. So if you are not at sea level, you probably have to make an adjustment.

If you're using the sheeting, or spoon, test, just know that the jelly syrup at first is light and runny and gets heavier as you cook it. The jelly will leave the spoon in a sheet, instead of separating into two or more droplets, when the jelling point is reached.

You have to skim any foam off the boiling syrup before you fill the jars. You can add a little butter or vegetable oil (like ½ teaspoon) to the fruit mixture before boiling to reduce the amount of foam.

Skim the jelly or jam after the sugar is in. Don't skim the boiling fruit—that isn't scum, it's just bubbles. It's the fruit that needs the cooking, incidentally, not the sugar, so that's why the fruit is boiled for some fifteen minutes before the sugar goes in.

Never squeeze or press the jelly bag to get the juice out of the fruit. It will make the jelly cloudy instead of clear. Sometimes it takes all night for the juice to drip through. You can make a jelly bag in the shape of a deep inverted cone out of muslin or flannel, or you can buy one. You can also drain the juice out through a few layers of cheesecloth.

If you're canning with antique jelly jars or old jelly glasses, you can't get new standard canning lids that fit them (and you can't process in a boiling water canner). So you have to use paraffin wax to seal them, which you melt over boiling water, and then pour about a ⅛-inch layer onto the jelly. But you have to wait till the jelly cools off a little, or the wax will pull away from the sides of the glass as the jelly cools. The paraffin should touch all the sides of the glass. If there are any air bubbles in the wax, prick them.

Go outside! If your jelly is undercooked—syrup, instead of jelly—you can always take off the lids and put it back in a saucepan, boil it up again and try for jelling a second time, maybe adding a cup of apple juice. However, in a very old jelly book, the writer suggested you put the jars out in the sun for the afternoon—the heat would keep activating the pectin. Just the opposite of what you'd think, like maybe you'd stick the jelly in the refrigerator to get it to harden. Make sure, however, that the problem isn't a lack of pectin; try this method only if your recipe has some apple juice, apples, or currants in it.

On pickles:

When making pickles, use stoneware, pottery, or glass bowls, and stain-less steel or enamelware cooking pans. Don't use cast iron or nonanodized aluminum bowls, cookware, or spoons.

If you want the liquid that the pickled vegetables are in to be clear, use distilled white vinegar, rather than the darker-colored cider vinegar or an herb-flavored vinegar. You can use cider vinegar in recipes where it doesn't matter if the vegetables darken, or if the brine is dark. Make sure the vinegar label, like the one on distilled white vinegar, says it's 5% acidity.

Don't ever substitute table salt for pickling salt. It contains anticaking agents that can make the pickling solution cloudy or leave a sediment in the jar. Iodine can darken pickles.

Give pickles in pint jars at least 15 minutes in the boiling water bath; make it 20 minutes if you're using quart jars. Store pickles while they ripen in a cool, dark, dry place. Don't try to make pickles with supermarket cucumbers that have a wax coating, and don't let the cucumbers sit for more than 24 hours after picking: they have to be really fresh and firm. That's true of any vegetable you're canning.

Trust this turn of events. Don't think you should be walking over there. Keep walking straight ahead. Whatever happens is going to be good.

ABOUT THE AUTHOR

Debby Bull is a former editor and writer for *Rolling Stone* magazine. She grew up in St. Croix Falls, Wisconsin. She graduated from Northwestern University and has a master's degree in American Studies from the University of Minnesota. As a rock critic and popular-culture observer, her writing has appeared in many magazines. She now lives in Montana and northern Wisconsin.